The Poems of Theocritus

The Poems of Theocritus

Translated with Introductions by
Anna Rist

THE UNIVERSITY OF NORTH CAROLINA PRESS
CHAPEL HILL

Copyright © 1978 by
The University of North Carolina Press
All rights reserved
Manufactured in the United States of America
Library of Congress Catalog Card Number 77-20042
ISBN 0-8078-1317-6

Library of Congress Cataloging in Publication Data

Theocritus.
  The poems of Theocritus.

  Bibliography: p.
  Includes index.
  I. Rist, Anna, 1936–
PA4443.E5R57   884'.01   77-20042
ISBN 0-8078-1317-6

φιλτάτῳ
ἀνδρῶν

❧ Contents

৯ Translator's Preface

The translations are the raison d'être of this work. They must be left to speak for themselves and, alas, within their limitations, for Theocritus. A translation, since it serves up an author strained, as it were, through another man's sieve, may prove as prejudicial to its origin as cabbage water to cabbage—something worse than no dish! Theocritus here appears in my rendering—it could not be otherwise—and I cannot pretend to have delivered him in anything like completeness. If I am thought to have transmitted some savour witheld by previous strainings, I must be satisfied. My hope is no more than to share what I admire in Theocritus, both as poet and as man, with some others with a taste for both poetry and humanity, but who cannot meet him in his own Greek tongue.

The General Introduction outlines my aims and methods in making the translation. It also seeks to place Theocritus in a literary and historical perspective and to record what little may be known or conjectured about the events of his life. Out of respect for my poet as well as my readers, I have not wished to deliver him to them at the outset neatly wrapped up in any pretence at a critical evaluation. This follows on my view that Theocritus is as open-ended as, for example, T. S. Eliot. I have preferred the method of indicating his character *ambulando*, in introductions to the individual poems, in the hope that he may emerge rather than be laid down, and that the reader may be in a better position to follow and to judge for himself as the evidence unfolds.

The introductions, besides their interpretative function, contain whatever factual material I have thought necessary to the reader's comprehension. I have normally assumed him to have access to a ready-reference work or annotated text such as that of K. J. Dover (unfortunately select) for such identifications of mythological or geographical names as he may feel himself in need of. As I wished this work to take on the character of a volume of poetry rather than a school textbook, I have avoided encumbering it with a glossary. The reader confronted, for example, with an obscure place name should not necessarily be expected to locate it, as it were, on a map, its locale being rather a terrain of the imagination. I believe this to be in the spirit of my original, who uses recherché references without creating any compulsion for his readers to fit them into more context than he provides or they desire. The very presence of a glossary creates this compulsion, and the need to keep a finger in the back of the book is inimical to a relaxed appreciation.

My own most constant source of information has been the great edition and commentary of A. S. F. Gow, the foundation on which is still being constructed the edifice of contemporary criticism to which the present work is both indebted and contributory. A select guide to this edifice is provided in my Bibliography. My translation is based on Gow's text with but rare departures, though it should be noted that my line numbers are not his. Also, I accept Gow's judgments (which are conservative) as to authenticity. Of the manuscript poems of Theocritus that are generally agreed to be spurious, VII, IX, and XXV can be found in the appendix; the others—XIX, XX, XXI, and XXIII—are not translated here. The interested reader will find the relevant scholarship in Gow, together with information and conclusions about the transmission of the text, which, as they do not directly concern translation or literary criticism of Theocritus, are not dealt with here except for passing mention in introductions to some individual poems. I proffer my interpretations of two controverted Idylls (XII and XXVI) as favourable both to their intelligibility and to their Theocritean authorship.

If Theocritus may at length be appreciated as more than the scholar's poet he has usually appeared to be, it will be in great part due to Gow's signal scholarship. If my conclusions as to literary interpretation not infrequently go beyond Gow's, it is no doubt due in part to my lack of scholarly caution. But it is apparent that in the unfolding of an ancient poet the scholar and the literary critic must join forces, each having respect for the other's work. I am bold enough to think that my interpretations, where they offer some new approach, may bear the examination of scholars and be of interest to them as well as to the general reader. There are also some obscure spots in the text for which I have offered renderings that I regard as at least plausible. These are (references to Gow's edition): II 60, III 29, 30, IV 11, IV 22, VI 18, XIII 15, XVIII 26, 27, XXIV 11, 12, XXVI 31, 32, XXIX 19, 20, XXX 20.

I am indebted to an array of scholarly authors who are acknowledged in footnotes. Among them Gilbert Lawall should receive special mention, for while I cannot accept as it stands the main thesis of his book, *Theocritus' Coan Pastorals*, I have made use of a number of insights of his regarding the first seven Idylls.

I am particularly grateful to Professor Richard Tarrant, who has painstakingly read the finished draft and drawn my attention to a fair crop of weak spots, besides making some useful suggestions on the arrangement of material in the General Introduction.

I further acknowledge with gratitude the Mellon Foundation's financial backing which has made publication possible, and the manifold co-operation of the personnel of The University of North Carolina Press, particularly in agreeing to the retention of my British spelling and punctuation.

Mrs. Susan Chisholm, by her patience in deciphering scrawled-over pages, has saved me many an hour of rewriting which I could ill spare. Under her hands the typescript finally emerged from chaos. At an earlier stage, the survival of my manuscript has depended on my husband, John M. Rist, whose skill in keeping control over stray notes is only one respect in which his virtues balance my deficiencies. This book owes to him its very coming into being. He first urged me to undertake it and has encouraged me through fully a decade of common domestic and professional vicissitudes, submitting with his ready good will and lively intellect to Theocritean confrontations in season and out. It is only one of the enterprises that without him I should hardly have entertained, let alone seen through to the end.

General Introduction

✽ General Introduction

The Greek literature traditionally denoted as Classical is typified by the writings of four Athenians of the fifth and fourth centuries B.C.: the dramatic works of Sophocles (496–406 B.C.), the history of Thucydides (460–ca. 400 B.C.), the philosophy of Plato (427–347 B.C.), and the political speeches of Demosthenes (383–322 B.C.). Of these and their contemporaries it is, with little reservation, fair to state that they view man in the setting that according to Aristotle (an exact contemporary of Demosthenes) is proper and natural to him, the autonomous Greek city-state (or *polis*) of the age. For them, 'nature' is an abstract term (*physis*) denoting the order of the cosmos or meaning the special and paramount case of human nature, particularly in antithesis to custom. Classical Greeks are, almost without exception, uninterested in nature in the wild.

In pursuit of the 'Father of Pastoral', Theocritus (born ca. 300 B.C.), we may put on one side the historical, political and even philosophical literature, of which the primary material is mundane events or phenomena, to concentrate our attention on the creative writing or poetry—the Greek *poiēsis* ('poesy') means a making or creation—of the Classical period that preceded him. Among the poetic productions of the age of which we have knowledge, poetic drama of one kind or another predominates overwhelmingly; indeed, little else has survived. The Classical period's most complete self-expression is found in its tragedy, as represented at its most typical by Sophocles and by the two other famous dramatists whose *floruit* merges with his, Aeschylus (525–456 B.C.) and Euripides (480–406 B.C.). The highly sophisticated Old Comedy has come down to us in the works

[3]

of Aristophanes (ca. 448–ca. 380 B.C.), and there is further an intermediary class of tragicomic drama of which no great amount survives. We have, in addition to complete or almost complete works (seven of Aeschylus, seven of Sophocles, eighteen of Euripides, and eleven of Aristophanes) citations and fragments of these and other authors, and descriptions or comments on works no longer extant.

In Classical tragedy, nature, its woods and rivers, and above all its mountains, is the frame for the *polis*, or at most is seen in relation to the events of the *polis*—as the locale of Oedipus' final purification, or of the gods' vengeance on Hippolytus. It is even an environment to be shunned by man, because it may bring him to be uncomfortably involved with its gods. Thus it is through hunting that Hippolytus becomes a votary of Artemis, and through meddling with Dionysus on the slopes of Cithaeron that Pentheus (in Euripides' *Bacchae*) becomes his victim. In Theocritus we shall view the reversal of this assumption, with nature the 'natural' setting for the operations of destiny *within* man.

Tragedy is the representative poetic genre of the Classical period, but comedy stands in a more likely-seeming relationship to Theocritus by literary descent, and, by its origins in Dionysiac ritual, has prima facie a closer connection with wild nature. However, the plays of Aristophanes show on this point no essential difference in outlook from that of tragedy, but only a difference of emphasis. They are, if anything, even more exclusively focussed upon man as the denizen of the *polis*, because they are unconcerned with his metaphysical situation and aim largely to criticize or merely poke fun at his habits and institutions, often with highly personal and local reference. Nature in Aristophanes is paraded as a handy vehicle for (personified) comment on the two-legged creature—and becomes in the process amusingly civilized.

That Greek Comedy after Aristophanes underwent an evolution so radical as to leave but scant trace of its relationship to the parent stock is as notorious as is the changeling's subsequent gestation of Roman and Renaissance Comedy. Much has been conjectured about the course of this evolution but little is known for certain. So far as we are concerned, the New Comedy, thin-blooded by comparison with the Old, and yet pregnant with a perduring vitality, emerges fully formed in Menander (ca. 342–292 B.C.), the only representative of whose plays any substantial portion has survived, though the genre survives also in its Latin imitators. We find that nature, the Aristophanic commentator on man, has been left behind, and that natural surroundings, such as lonely hillsides or the sea, are chiefly valuable insofar as they make possible such human vicissitudes as shipwrecks or the abandoning and finding of babies. This, though it brings us a stage nearer to Theocritus and European Pastoral (as well as European Comedy, to which, in the Renaissance, the Pastoral is found related)—since the finders of infants are likely to be ob-scure countrymen such as shepherds—seems even further away from Theocritus, so far as attention to nature itself is concerned.

Returning, for a more general view, to tragedy as the repre-sentative poetic genre of the Classical Period, we note that the conflicts which form the tragedian's subject are typically viewed as clashes of human reason and duty with a controlling fate that even the gods subserve. In Aeschylus the human group appears rather as clan than as the full-blown *polis*, and the forces of destiny have a certain primitive moral grandeur inspiring confi-dence. In Sophocles they appear still family-linked, but strik-ingly less moral in any man-based sense, and concomitantly more inexorable. We understand 'justice' to be defined by the superior 'necessity' itself. In Euripides, man (the 'political ani-mal' of Aristotle) is, albeit impotently, in revolt, and his individ-ual intimate feelings themselves claim and deserve a hearing —by men and by such gods as may be disposed to sympathy. There is a strong sense that justice is indeed what man under-stands by it, but that the superior order (embodied in the gods) often distinctly and arbitrarily flouts it and thereby invites man's hatred more than his gratitude.

Undoubtedly the most promising link between Theocritus and Classical Greek literature is to be found in Euripides—and in the light of this conclusion, Theocritus' short poem on the subject of the great playwright's *Bacchae* assumes a particular significance. But Euripides, revolutionary though contemporaries such as Aristophanes found him, and seminal to the Greco-Roman mind for many centuries as we know him to have been (he was long used as text for comment in schools, and this pedagogic prestige accounts for the survival of so comparatively many of his plays), cannot ultimately be dissociated from the two other outstanding tragic writers of fifth-century Athens. When everything has been said about the differences between the three (which here have been only broadly indicated), there remains an overriding comparability of outlook in the polarization of the universe between man and the powers above. By Theocritus (though with no little impetus from Euripides, who initiates a thrust in this direction) the gap is so narrowed that the polarity is minimal, the fatal powers very close to man's own bosom, if not within it. The tendency to view individual man as a subject, begun in Euripides, is complete, and with it goes his placement into the natural setting from which he emerges, rather than into the political setting which arises from his own nature. For this radical modification, the political evolution of the Greek world between the fourth and third centuries B.C. has made way.

THE POLITICAL BACKGROUND

If we turn to Thucydides and Demosthenes, it will be to read how the distinctive traditional modes subtending the political entity of each *polis* and based upon tensions more or less precariously maintained, failed, in the field of external relations, to withstand the jealousies and antagonisms engendered as the more powerful states proceeded with expansion in accordance with their own conceptions of their national destiny, and smaller ones, whether through weakness or ambition, became involved in the power struggle. The internal cohesion collapsed as factions arose, and the long series of agonies that we call the Peloponnesian War (431–404 B.C.)—surely one of the saddest episodes in history and the most instructive as to human nature—had the only outcome of weakening the vitality of the *polis* and its cultural life.

A craving for a wider identity already makes itself heard in the speeches of the Athenian rhetor Isocrates (436–338 B.C.). Meanwhile, apprehension at the growing insolence of the kingdom of Macedon to the north—a Greek people, but to Athenians little better than barbarians—can be gauged from Demosthenes' diatribes against the Macedonian king, Philip. Yet it was Philip's son, Alexander, who was to give direction and substance to the developing instinct for Panhellenism. His fabled accumulation of conquests (336–323 B.C.) revived the Persian concept of empire and foreshadowed the Roman *imperium* (Alexander became, indeed, Julius Caesar's conscious model), bringing as it did the same requisites for its administration: an efficient system of communications, a bureaucracy, and a *lingua franca*.

But this monumental unity survived only as long as its founder. After Alexander's premature death, there was a period of indecision which ended in 301 B.C. with the battle fought at Ipsus, in Phrygia. The empire was parcelled out into the hands of the conqueror's aides, and three lines of *diadochi* ('successors') eventually established themselves in Pella, Antioch, and Alexandria. There opened the Hellenistic Age, in which Greek culture became widespread and, though in character exclusive, began, particularly in the domain of religion, and derivatively therefore in art, to assimilate some Oriental and Egyptian elements.

The influential centres were the seats and outposts of autocracies absorbed by the external power game and the internal exigencies of making their yoke felt and accepted over broad territories of often non-Greek inhabitants. Here we must focus on the most powerful and prestigious of these kingdoms, that of the general Ptolemy, comprising Egypt, Libya, and the lower part of Syria, since it includes the environment in which Theocritus passed all his productive life. The realm of Seleucus was larger, consisting of the greater part of Alexander's vast conquests eastward to the Indus; but the very size of the domain made for a decentralized administration, and the ruling caste of Macedonians, to whom had quickly been added a host of other

Greek settlers, was scattered far afield. In Ptolemy's realm they centred on the city founded by Alexander, and named for him, on the westernmost arm of the Nile delta.

Until Rome's zenith, Alexandria was to eclipse all western cities by the magnificence of its structures and the brilliance of its court-centred society. It was a planned city, laid out in blocks in the manner introduced by Hippodamus, the architect of Piraeus, in the mid-fifth century. Its twin harbours were artificially divided by a mole seven stades long (1400 yards), leading out to the island of Pharos, on which stood the famous lighthouse. On the shores of the eastward harbour lay the spacious Royal Quarters, comprising the Palace and ancillary buildings. Here successive Ptolemies were laid in their tombs, and here the body of Alexander was brought by his general's son, the second of the dynasty, and interred in a monument of great splendour. Here, too, the first Ptolemy, toward the end of his reign (323–283 B.C.), built and endowed the 'House of the Muses', the Museum, with stipends for poets and pedants enough to amass there the treasury of extant learning and letters to which the history of civilization must ever after acknowledge itself indebted. The storehouse of all this treasure, the Library, was envisaged in the original plan but built by his successor, the most brilliant and powerful monarch of the line, Ptolemy II. The poet Callimachus (whose first Hymn contrives to pay a double tribute to the rulers both of heaven and of earth, and ends with a double prayer for the goods within their respective gift, virtue and riches) was raised from the lowly position of schoolmaster to an exalted one in the royal patronage. Under Ptolemy's generous protection, he not only maintained a large output of highly polished and erudite verses, but wrote a catalogue of the new library: 120 volumes of information and criticism on the contents of the books and their authors. With this royal benignity we have to contrast the cruel death meted out to another poet, Sotades, who opened his mouth too frankly on the subject of Ptolemy's second marriage, to his sister, Arsinoë II. Sister-marriage, practised by the former rulers of Egypt, the Pharoahs, and having probably a religious significance in the conservation of the blood royal, was abhorred by

the Greeks as incest. We shall find Theocritus in his court pan-
egyric, Idyll XVII, circumspectly referring to this aspect of the
monarch's life by an irreproachable comparison with the wed-
ding of the children of Cronus, Zeus and Hera. That Theocritus'
contact with Alexandria falls within the reign of the second
Ptolemy is clear from this poem, the 'Encomium', as also from
the other Alexandrian Idyll, XV, with its reference to the deifica-
tion of the wife of Ptolemy I, Berenice, which took place during
the reign of her son and daughter. A third Alexandrian poem,
the 'Berenice', is lost but for a fragment.

THE LIFE OF THEOCRITUS

An outline of Theocritus' career may be very broadly inferred
from the poems themselves, for the brief biographical accounts
that have been handed down are in conflict and seem themselves
to be largely inferential. One statement, that he was a native of
Syracuse, seems borne out by his own words at XI 5 and XXVIII
31, and may be accepted as substantial. Moreover, it makes
readily intelligible the choice of the rising star, Hiero, as the
subject of his first appeal for patronage, Idyll XVI. That failing,
he must have turned with less enthusiasm—witness the con-
ventional praises of Idyll XVII, and the contrast with the easy
humour of Idyll XVI—to the sun of suns in Egypt and taken up
his residence in Alexandria.

Prior to the appeal to Hiero, Theocritus must have passed
some years on the island of Cos, the locality that has the richest
associations in his poems and forms the setting for the key
'autobiographical' Idyll, VII (see the introduction to that poem).
That Idyll, too, may provide the clue to his going to Cos in the
mention of the master poet Philetas who lived there with his
circle. Since Philetas was dead by 283 B.C., the placing of Theo-
critus' *floruit* in the 124th Olympiad (284–280 B.C.) is another
detail which we may accept from the biographies. The city of
Cos boasted a famous medical school, which makes it plausible
that it was there that Theocritus struck up his friendship with
Nicias, a young man of about his own age, as appears from his

manner of addressing him in Idylls IX and XIII. In Idyll XXVIII, a late poem, we find Nicias married and settled in medical practice in Miletus, where Theocritus has, it seems, visited him; but this is well after the Alexandrian interlude. Several of the bucolic Idylls may have been composed during these Coan Years: I, III, and VI suggest themselves as relatively early. The scene of Idyll II is most probably the shoreward outskirts of the city of Cos, but the poem would appear to be a later production and to be classed with the mimes, Idylls XIV and XV. Idyll XIII suggests what we know of Philetas and his romantic treatment of epic themes. Two bucolic Idylls, IV and V, are set in southern Italy, and as their realism and sophisticated characterization place them apart from the previous group—and also suggest the inclusion with them of Idyll X—it is possible that they were written there or in Sicily, if we assume Theocritus returned there from Cos at the time of his appeal to Hiero. This last event can be fairly safely dated to the period of Hiero's Generalship (275–269 B.C.), before he took the official title of king (see introduction to Idyll XVI); this leaves time for the Alexandrian 'Encomium' to be composed after the marriage of Ptolemy and Arsinoë II in 275 B.C. and before the queen's death in 270.

   The residence in Alexandria appears to have been of only two or three years' duration. Idyll XVII already betrays Theocritus as not at his ease in the climate of oriental adulation with which Ptolemy II had surrounded himself. Idyll XIV, though it forms a mimetic pair with XV, is not set in Alexandria, and the worked-in tribute to Ptolemy which concludes it contains one not un-ambiguous phrase which has been interpreted as suggesting a measure of disillusion (but see p. 127). Now if Idyll II is to be dated to the same period as these other mimes—and its dramatic power and penetrating psychological insight certainly call for a later dating than the early bucolic Idylls with which an inferior manuscript tradition has classed it—then we may presume Theocritus to have retired from Alexandria to the city and island of his predilection—a tactful withdrawal from the sun's full glare, since Ptolemy also favoured the island of his birth (see Idyll XVII). The love songs to boys, Idylls XXIX and XXX, indicate maturity of age, and they, as well as Idyll XXVIII, are written in Sapphic metres, a break from the epic hexameter which was Theocritus' own contribution to the conventions of small-scale poetry. After this period, to which we must also assign the stay in Miletus presupposed by Idyll XXVIII, Theocritus' voice is no more heard.

THEOCRITUS AND HELLENISTIC POETRY

Poetic form that we regard as typically Hellenistic came about in part as a result of the feeling that the quasi-canonical epic vein had been worked out by the incomparable Homer, and that henceforth life must be scrutinized, and art synthesized, in miniature, from the vast treasury of information amassed by critic and grammarian. Some poets might cling to the lengthy epic as their medium—the *Thebaid* of Antimachus of Colophon, a century previous to Theocritus, was a notorious and influential example—but in their hands the heroic tale became a pretext for endless learned digressions, which to the age of the ready-reference book seem merely pedantic as poetry. When Lycidas, in Idyll VII, scorns 'those cuckoos of the Muses who sing in emulation of the bard of Chios [Homer]', he has in mind the followers of Antimachus, as exemplified particularly in the contemporary Apollonius of Rhodes (for whom see the introduction to Idyll XIII). So in the same poem Simichidas aligns himself with upholders of the small-scale-and-high-polish school of poetry, Asclepiades of Samos (Sicelides is his known pseudonym) and Philetas, who was perhaps the chief inducement for Theocritus' sojourn on the island of Cos, the scene of this same Idyll. Three poems of Theocritus have come down to us which are to be classified as 'epyllia', illustrating, as they do, the handling of epic material in the short form prescribed by Callimachus, the literary arbiter of the age. The probable relationship of two of them to the contemporary controversy is examined in the introductions to Idylls XIII and XXII. Idyll XXIV, as explained in its introduction, is perhaps a special case.

Theocritus' specific importance in the history of literature rests on his invention (early asserted and nowhere contradicted) of the genre we know as the 'bucolic idyll'—terms which here require explanation. 'Bucolic' strictly relates to cowherds (Greek *boukolos*), but is used by Theocritus both in the strict sense (as of Daphnis in Idyll I) and to refer to herdsmen and rustics in general, in the same way as, in later times, the term 'pastoral' lost its strict association with shepherds (Latin *pastor*) and came (with 'bucolic') to be applied to the countryside viewed in the idyllic tradition fathered unwittingly by Theocritus.

The Greek word 'idyll' (*eidyllion*) must be taken to mean something like 'little picture'. It is related to 'ideal' (Greek *idea*), and this fact is noteworthy since the poetic form is characterized, even in Theocritus, by an idealizing tendency. Later associations of 'ideal' are, of course, founded on Plato, and it is far from clear to what extent these associations may have influenced the earliest use of the word 'idyll' in a literary context. So far as we know, the word is not to be ascribed to Theocritus himself; it is first found in a commentator and comes into common usage only in later Roman times. However, the thing it denotes, the 'little picture' itself, is peculiar to the Hellenistic Age, being approved by Callimachus and practised by him in his *Epigrams*. Theocritus' poetic technique produces a visual effect, a scene composed of fine detail, and is comparable in this to the contemporary plastic and pictorial arts with their highly imaginative choices of subject and dramatic capturing of the fleeting moment. Well-known examples which have been compared to figures 'depicted' in Theocritus' idylls are the aged fisherman in the Louvre, the thorn-puller in the Vatican galleries, and the seated boxer in the Terme Museum in Rome. (Cf. Idylls I, IV, XXII respectively.) Often one 'picture' is superimposed on another by the juxtaposition of motifs of high imaginative impact that are particularly visual in quality, though the appeal to the ear is constantly there also.

Theocritus' most obvious poetic device, and one which comes almost to characterize the bucolic convention, is that of the song, or the song contest, set within the poem, which extends, more or less at will, the poet's scope. The description of the cup in Idyll I is an example drawn from another art form, and the specification of scenery or 'props' (as the statue of Priapus in I, the cave mouth in III, and the imaginative evocations of Bourina Spring and the scene of the harvest festival in VII) is another tool of the same technique. The reader is required to intuit the poem's unity from the amalgam of suggestivities, a task requiring alertness and some labour, and suited in this to Hellenistic tastes, as also perhaps to our own.

The bucolic idyll, and the long tradition it innovated, is designed to illustrate human attitudes and dilemmas within a conventionalized small-scale setting of country life and manners. The most common theme explored is that of Eros, and the painful paradoxes he (the personifying god) poses for men: fidelity of the spirit against the temptation of concupiscence (Idyll I); the lover's powerlessness to compel a response (II, III, and Simichidas' song in Idyll VII); lubriciousness and sentiment as attitudes inhabiting the same mind (IV); while Idylls V and VI display respectively the animosity generated by lust and the harmony of a love in which body and spirit both have their place. The list may be extended: Eros' deceptive power (X); his enfeebling effect on body and mind (I, II, XI); the lover's recourse to strategy and pretence (VI). However, Theocritus, as we see, is not presenting an ethical disquisition with the illustrative details subordinated to a grand design, but a significant arrangement of related vignettes—more like a Roman mosaic than a Persian carpet; and this mode of depiction, if truthful, must suggest more than its author himself consciously comprehends. (So T. S. Eliot, who employed a comparable method, is said to have expressed gratitude to his critics for 'explaining' his work to him—and they may be kept busy at their task for some time to come!) For this reason Theocritus is likely to remain to a degree elusive— quite apart from the consideration that we must labour to recreate the connotations that even ordinary references would have had for men living in Theocritus' own environment. Moreover, he tends to be deliberately and fashionably allusive and recondite, in a manner calculated to tease the discernment of cultured Alexandrians.

To designate one man as the father of an art form is not to

imply that it sprang fully formed from his brain, a new creation, but rather that certain elements, appearing incidentally in the work of predecessors or contemporaries, and responding to some temper of the age, are fused by the alchemy of a particular personality in time and space into a new and 'typical' form. The poet (from a Greek word meaning 'maker') may be virtually unconscious of creating a new form, and indeed while it remains in his hands it may not appear as anything so stereotyped, its defining lines being ever the bounds of a living personality. By imitators of lesser spiritual stature or a totally different caste of personality, it will be welcomed chiefly for the discipline it offers to their immature muses and for its proven success value. So it will tend to congeal, until some native fire of genius transform it. In the evolution of time, this was to befall the pastoral tradition itself, as when Milton poured his inner struggles and those of his nation and creed into the mold of the First Idyll.

We know that contemporary poets are named by Theocritus in Idyll VII—a context which invites us to assume their influence upon him. Of these, Philetas sang of the countryside, as did a pupil of Asclepiades, Hermesianax. Not that we find before Theocritus any sure indication of its treatment as a microcosm for the observation of human manners and destiny. Individual names apart, turning to the countryside for peace and reflection was a natural impulse of the age, which we may term escapist if we will. The contemporary cultured Greek, the professional man or the bureaucrat caught up in the administrative machinery of one or other of the Hellenistic kingdoms, could raise his eyes, in imagination at least, to the limitless horizons of mountain and plain, forest and pasture, and to the contemplation of lives passed obscurely, or amid a merely local prestige won by personal worth or accomplishment, in the pursuit of rustic skills and nourished by a wholesome country air: free from the corruptions of wealth and power and the rumours of wars which clouded the centres of civilization. It is a fact that herdsmen did (as they still in remote parts of Europe do) while away their time in singing and playing on instruments and in poetic composition, and that they might not infrequently perform these activities in concert or in competition with one another. No doubt many a local reputation was established, and some in time became legendary; while mythical prototypes (such as, in Sicily particularly, Daphnis) would have been invoked both as matter and as patrons, or even authors, for such songs. The practice had become an inveterate literary tradition; its *locus classicus* was Hesiod's account, at the opening of his *Works and Days*, of how he received the poetic gift while herding on the slopes of Mount Helicon (see introduction to Idyll VII). Thus it seems probable that the critical source of Theocritus' originality was the working out of this literary convention in terms of a revived appreciation, in recent life and literature, for the real pleasures of the countryside, combined with the actual customs of herdsmen, known to him from his Sicilian background and his travels in southern Italy and the Aegean. In particular, these must have provided what became, as we have seen, a distinguishing feature of the bucolic idyll—the song and the song contest.

While Theocritus' longer poems are in general referred to as Idylls and described as bucolic, it is contended that three (II, XIV, and XV) belong to the classification of the mime, and that of these, two are not in any sense bucolic. A mime is a short *dramatic* representation of realistic scenes, usually (though not in the case of Idyll XIV) from urban life, for the most part humorous, often bawdy. A mime does not seem necessarily or even usually intended to be acted. Idyll XV, however, can be performed with great effect. I have not heard of a performance of Idyll XIV, but imagine it could form a diverting enough interlude. Idyll II, being a soliloquy, would require a virtuoso.

In Theocritus' works one can in fact observe the easy transition from the pastoral idyll, characterized by its song-motif, through the 'amoebean' Idyll V, in which speaking parts are assigned and merge into song, or the monologue Idyll III, which also contains song—to the mime, whose characteristics I have enumerated. In fact the step is short to Idyll XIV, with its part rural background, from the agricultural Idyll X, with its exchange of songs, though this is usually classed with the pastorals. Both represent the interchange of two men on the subject of the desire of one of them for a woman; both conclude with counsels for diverting the mind from its malaise.

Comparisons have been sought between the mimes of Theocritus and those of Herondas, his near contemporary and the chief surviving representative of the genre. Such results as the search has yielded will receive mention in the introduction to Idyll XV, to which they relate, and which—as will have appeared above—is the only poem of Theocritus thoroughly to qualify for the title of mime. The most obvious difference between the two is in the last characteristic mentioned—bawdiness. While Herondas' mimes are in every sense vulgar—and proceed from the satirist's impulse to lay the seamy side of ordinary life open to ridicule—the response Theocritus evokes is sympathetic, even while he invites laughter, as in Idylls XIV and XV (Idyll II is only marginally risible).

That there should be a resemblance between attitudes characteristic of the mime and those of the contemporary comedy is only what we should expect. The relationship accounts for the surprise of recognition that certain scenes, characters, and even words may occasion in a modern reader familiar with Renaissance Comedy, for the latter, via the Roman comedies of Plautus and Terence, goes back to Greek roots. And there may be a further factor at work, a certain temperamental kinship between Theocritus and Shakespeare. At all events, I am unable to read Idyll XIV without hearing echoes of the subplot of *Twelfth Night* in the drinking party, with its banter, puns, and snatches of song. Thyonichus' gibing references to the 'Pythagorist'—which he probably uses as a general term for an itinerant ascetic or freak—even recall the Puritan Malvolio, whose rigorism, though proof against 'cakes and ale', fell so easy a victim to an eros not for wheaten bread. And we are surely on firm ground in recognizing in both Aeschinas and Sir Toby Belch that pertinacious anti-hero the *miles gloriosus*.

THE PRESENT TRANSLATION

The most prominent feature of Theocritus' language is his use of the Doric dialect traditional to his native Sicily, in an age when the common speech (*koinē*) of the civilized world (*oikoumenē*) was of Attic descent—of which the representative best known to most people today is the language of the New Testament. The Doric dialect might be represented in English by a Burnsesque Scots, except that it was better established as a literary form of Greek and more easily transliterated into the common tongue; indeed, Doric forms were a regular feature of the choruses of tragedies. The dialect would not, therefore, present a comparable impediment to the readers to whom Theocritus' poems were addressed, who, since their fashion was to pride themselves on an elitist cultivation, would rather savour the antique and rustic Doric, with its broad vowels, as an added relish. Interlarded with the Doric are words and phrases reminiscent of Homer, the traditional poetic change of all Greek speakers. Not surprisingly, this seasoning is heaviest in the poems dealing with old epic themes, Idylls XIII, XXII, and XXIV.

Theocritus' verse as a whole is highly poetic, in the Greek sense that minimized the distinction between poetry and song. The aural effect is carefully managed. Indeed, as we have seen, a Theocritean artifice is to overlay poetry with song; and, with less artifice, the interspersion of lays sung by fictitious minstrels into the performances of actual rhapsodes is a convention dating back at least to the Homeric poems. From Homer on, Greek poetry was recited in a singsong chant, whether to an audience or privately, and the Greeks clearly developed a discriminating ear for sounds. In illustration of this may be cited an incident which became a standing joke in fifth-century Athens. An actor delivering the words *galến' horō* ('I see a calm') distorted the pitch of the final syllable of *galēn'*, thereby producing *galễn* ('a polecat') and bringing into uproar an audience composed of both sexes and all classes of citizens. It was matter for marvel that Euripides read silently, only moving his lips. St. Augustine, in the fourth century A.D., still finds noteworthy the same feat performed by Bishop Ambrose of Milan. I have attempted to render Theocritus' aurally highly wrought lines into comparably euphonious English, and also to maintain some equivalence of their recherché and archaic spicing without obscuring the fresh and often highly realistic impact of Theocritus' verse. Constant attention has also been paid to representing the sound quality of the original where it underscores the poignancy, tenderness, or delicacy of many human scenes or descriptions of nature or art. Mindful of the linguistic parallel between our own day, when English is becoming the *koinē* of the *oikoumenē*, and that of Theocritus, I have thought fit to season my idiom, unfashionably, with the occasional poeticism. While I hope by restraint not to violate the democratic susceptibilities of the age, I think this the only way of conveying something of the esoteric character of Theocritus' chosen style.

As to metre, the hexameter line normally used by Theocritus in the *Idylls* is itself an innovation, being traditionally tied to the Greek epic. Callimachus' epigrams are in elegiac couplets, which became the dominant form for shorter poems in both Greek and Latin. If care is taken to sound the English renderings 'on the inward ear', in the manner required by the verse of Hopkins (in default of reading aloud), they will be found to express themselves in regular lines of four, five, or six pronounced (that is, lengthened or emphasized) syllables. I allowed myself this latitude in rendering Theocritus' hexameters, as regard to other features of the individual poem seemed to cast it more naturally into one or the other line. The guiding principle has been to sacrifice, where appropriate, consistency in rendering the form, in a bid for Theocritean ease and harmony of flow.

To the above general account of my proceeding, there are both metrical and dialectic exceptions to be found among the *Idylls*. Idylls XXVIII, XXIX, and XXX are, as already mentioned, in metres used by Sappho. The three love poems, Idylls XII, XXIX, and XXX, are in the Aeolic dialect. I have not found it practical to render these distinctions.

Since some savour of the original is inevitably lost in the transition from language to language (and how much more from an ancient language whose word associations are imperfectly known to us), I have not scrupled to compensate for this literary entropy by exploiting, from time to time, possible English significances not strictly 'in the Greek'—an expediency I regard as higher fidelity to the original and an indispensable part of the translator's art. Some examples are: the ambiguity of 'determined on' in Idyll I; the various senses of 'licks' in III (which make it the appropriate word for the transition from animal to fire metaphor); in the same passage, 'witch' (the double English sense doing duty for the highly variable colouring of the Greek word, with, here, its magic–erotic overtones—cf. 'sorceress' at XIV 9); the idiomatic 'stick in your throat' at the end of the same poem (which, without being an exact rendering of the Greek, fits the character of the speaker); the adaptation of the English proverbial 'chip of the old block' for a similar and quite likely proverbial expression at X 7; 'grins' at XI 30 (a succinct treatment, more natural to English, of a Greek circumlocution); the drawing out at XIII 33 of the imagery latent in the Greek word for 'hollow' and the general context of the personified treatment of the ship Argo, to give 'Argo's womb'; the expression 'hour of trial', with its appropriate heroic overtones, for a simple Greek participle at XXII 78.

The Idylls

Idyll I

This poem stands first in all the extant collections. Whether, as is possible, this reflects Theocritus' own decision or rather that of an early editor,* it is easily seen to be appropriate. Idyll I, passing from 'actual' (idealized) characters through pictorial evocations of man's life to climax in the theme of the archetypal rustic hero, Daphnis, may be said to map out the terrain to be explored in the new bucolic mode. This terrain has always a double aspect: nature relating to man and man to nature. The point of interaction is man's propensities and passions, whether seen as noble or selfish, pathetic or revolting, absurd or merely trivial. Imposing themselves on nature they are art; mastering his psyche they are (as they are for that latter-day bucolic *poiētēs*, Thomas Hardy) fate. They *are* the forces of nature, more or less personified, which control his destiny and may impel him tragically to death or to that worse destruction which is his own denaturing. Theocritus' outlook thus reveals itself as a self-contained humanism, and in holding it the Sicilian of the third century B.C. shows himself as Greek as Sophocles. Only the mode has changed: the confined stage with its set scene is replaced by an imaginative canvas unrolling fugitive episodes and vistas.

Here, at the outset, Theocritus devises for us the 'idyllic' qualities of friendship and ceremony in the encounter between the humble, unnamed goatherd and the shepherd Thyrsis, who has 'brought to perfection the bucolic art'. We see their simple code of manners among men and of respect for their gods. They will be rudely parodied in the encounter in Idyll v. The landscape depicted in their words is the type of all subsequent idyllic landscapes, with its shade and running water to cool the noonday

*See the introduction to Idyll vi.

heat, and the simple embellishments of human craft: a rustic seat
and a statue of that god who personifies the most obvious com-
mon denominator of beasts and men, the simply sexual Priapus.
Art of a higher degree, not merely ordering nature but bodying
forth man's self-awareness—the respect in which he is unlike
the beasts—is also a prominent theme of this as of other Idylls.
The carving on the wooden bowl that the goatherd will present
to Thyrsis as a fit reward for singing a particularly celebrated
number from his repertory is described, with a pictorial elabo-
rateness highly agreeable to the tastes of Theocritus' age and
cultivated circle, in a passage which in length counterbalances
the song that follows. There are depicted three Ages of Man, no
doubt in a symmetrical arrangement of figures, the three 'vign-
ettes' being conventionally framed by borders of vines: a boy,
flanked by two foxes, absorbed in his hobby and oblivious of
the menace they constitute; two youths flanking a woman who
here represents the perverse eros, and obsessed to exhaustion
with their courtship of her; and—the central figure—an elderly
man intent on the occupation by which he must live.* The
whole thus presents the theme of a progressive engagement of
psychic energies in the realistic business of life, or, as we might
say, of a 'satisfactory adjustment'.

The poem climaxes in Thyrsis' song which opens with a verse
'signature', an establishment of copyright. Since existing ex-
planations have not succeeded in accounting for all the data and
a new approach is indicated, I offer the following construction,
psychological in its emphasis, of their relation to the present
matter. Behind the theme lies a body of Sicilian legends about
the folk-hero Daphnis. He was the son of a water nymph and in
infancy was 'exposed' (i.e., abandoned: see General Introduc-
tion, p. 5) under a laurel bush (*daphnē*), from which he derived
his name. A foundling, then, he grew up in close association
with nature, a cowherd by occupation and a master musician—
in all things the model for the new art form and for its characters

*Here I follow in the main the interpretation of Gilbert Lawall, *Theocritus'
Coan Pastorals*, Publications of the Center for Hellenic Studies, vol. 1 (Cam-
bridge: Harvard University Press, 1967), pp. 27–30.

and exponents (such as Thyrsis here) and a legend even to the graceless Lacon of Idyll V. In youth, Daphnis was loved by a nymph to whom he promised fidelity. Such a vow of continence, exceeding the natural capacity of man, constituted a challenge to Eros (the god Desire, whose target is the human breast, whereas his mother, Aphrodite, presides over the fecundating drives of all nature), who thereupon caused Daphnis to be tormented with sexual desire for a human girl (probably the Xenea —the name means 'Stranger'—of Idyll VII) and to be made drunk and seduced by her. In punishment for this breach of his promise he was blinded, and this aspect of the legends may be referred to in Priapus' speech, though it is not in evidence elsewhere in Thyrsis' song.

At the song's outset, we learn that the girl is seeking Daphnis; but he has resumed obedience to his vow and is refusing further intercourse with her, thus carrying the contest with Eros to another stage. This struggle against Desire (which we, dispensing with the mythology which for Theocritus is in any case largely dramatic personification, will prefer to locate *within* the human psyche) is physically exhausting him and we are told that he is 'wasting'—sitting or lying on the ground with his flocks at his feet, visited by wild animals and mourned by that nature (cf. Idyll VII) whose foster child he is. Nature is, indeed, the ground of his divided existence, in which gentle birth and upbringing are pitted against appetitive and destructive forces, and in this, as Theocritus means us to understand, he typifies all men.

Like Prometheus in Aeschylus' play, Daphnis is visited in his extremity by various gods, all in their own ways uncomprehending. First comes Hermes, patron of flocks and herdsmen, whose notion is simple and inadequate: Daphnis is clearly pining for love, and the puzzling intensity must relate to its object. Next is Priapus, demon of crude sexuality, who holds out the obvious remedy, couched in appropriately obscene terms.* Like

---

*The words of Priapus that I have rendered 'star-crossed' (with its associations for English readers with Romeo's perverse fate) and 'hapless' have been much discussed. The perversity with which Priapus twits Daphnis is, I be-

Prometheus, Daphnis remains silent; these tentatives do not touch his real situation. Finally comes Aphrodite, who knows what is going on and pretends solicitude, but finds Daphnis' determination secretly amusing, like the whim of a child. On her his contempt bursts out in hatred and abuse; she is the 'enemy of man', and he returns her veiled taunt with interest, reminding her of the less creditable episodes in her career—the liaison with Anchises, a cowherd like himself; the seduction of Adonis, another nature hero; and the wound she received from Diomedes before Troy. We must suppose Aphrodite surprised rather than angered, for as Daphnis sinks in exhaustion, she tries to raise him up, but, after bidding farewell to his life of the pastures and of music, he dies calling on nature to witness to the monstrosity of his plight.

The manner of Daphnis' death is left somewhat obscure; it is connected with a river, which must evoke the river of death, Acheron, but less generally suggests a feature of some of the legendary material: the final assimilation of Daphnis to the stream of his lover the nymph—or, if we wish to 'de-allegorize', the triumph of the gentle nature within man and the vanquishing of Eros prophesized by Daphnis in his reply to Aphrodite. Another legend related that the blind Daphnis wandered over a cliff, and some have wanted to take the river here as the literal cause of his death by drowning in the River Anapus, said in line 74 to have been deserted by the nymphs*. But Daphnis' blindness, if it is implied at all, is de-emphasized in Thyrsis' song, and he is certainly not wandering, since he is too weak to be raised to his feet. If Daphnis drowns, it is in a manner several degrees more metaphorical than the drowning of Hylas, who in Idyll XIII is drawn down into their pool to dwell with the nymphs who have fallen in love with him.

---

lieve, not that of simple infidelity or lust (attested senses of the Greek) but that of manufacturing (Romeo-like) his own ill fate and then acquiescing in it, instead of accepting it as given and acting directly to gratify his desires, 'like any sane man'.

*See R. M. Ogilvie's 'The Song of Thyrsis', *Journal of Hellenic Studies* 82 (1962):106–110; Ogilvie raises some important considerations.

To my mind, Theocritus is willing to be vague, playing on the legendary inconsistency and the various associations of 'river'. Characteristically, he is more concerned with the consistency of the internal action, the psychology of Daphnis' fate, than with the external events. Daphnis' death is *both* wanton *and* inevitable, both a punishment and a choice. It is paid to satisfy some complete order of the universe, but it is even in one sense satisfying to the victim. The last line of the song suggests that by it his fidelity is vindicated, his fault atoned.

Onto a setting of simple beauty in nature, art, and human friendliness, Theocritus has superimposed the tragic conflict of nature in man, at once generous and egocentric in its pulls, and suggests that the struggle for integrity and nobility is to the death, against a tyranny whose seat is in man's own breast. Those gods associated with nature and the herdsman's life are sympathetic but circumscribed in their influence and powerless to help beyond their own sphere. Even Priapus is relatively harmless, remaining within the landscape; his interest is in physical potency merely. It is those gods who embody the restive preying of desire upon life and the values toward which it would tend, Aphrodite and her son, who spoil life's harmony, though —as Theocritus, I think, would wish us to conclude—they provide the matter and the stimulus to the higher art by which men may transcend themselves and find a precarious atonement.

Thyrsis or The Song

(Thyrsis and a goatherd)

THYRSIS
Sweet music, goatherd, the pine by the spring yonder
makes with its whispering: sweet, too, your fluting,
and worthy to win second prize after Pan.
If his prize is the horned goat, you'll take the nanny;
if the nanny's for him, the kid falls to you;
kid's flesh is good eating, till the time you must milk her.

GOATHERD
Sweeter, shepherd, your song than the gushing
water that pours from the high rock yonder.
If the Muses bear off the ewe as their guerdon,
10   you'll take the lamb that's bred within doors;
if their choice is the lamb, you'll take the ewe after.

THYRSIS
I pray by the nymphs, goatherd, will you sit
on the slope of the hillock, there by the tamarisks,
and play on your pipe, while I mind your goats?

GOATHERD
Shepherd, I may not, for reverence of Pan,
pipe in the noonday; at that hour he rests,
worn out with the hunt. He is wrathful if roused;
the bitter bile sits on his nostril alway.
But you, Thyrsis, sing the sorrows of Daphnis,
20   and have brought to perfection the bucolic art!
Come, sit we under this elm tree, facing
the nymphs and Priapus there by the rustics'
seat and the oaks. If you sing as once,
competing with Chromis of Libya, I'll give you
to milk three times a she-goat with twins;
although she's two kids, she fills up two pails.

Plus an ivy-wood bowl, fragrant with wax,
two-handled, new-made: you can still smell the chisel.
High up, round the rim, twines ivy with sprays
of gold helichryse,* and all down the handles,   30
brave with its burden, the tendril winds on.
Within is a woman—the gods surely wrought her—
fine-woven her headband and robe. On each hand
stands a fair-bearded man, competing in turn
with words for her favour; her mind is unmoved:
now she looks at one, laughing, then on the other
casts her regard. Love has drawn circles
under their eyes; they labour in vain.
Beside these, an old fisherman is depicted.
He stands on a scaly rock, labours to drag   40
his net to the cast—the picture of toil!
You would swear he was fishing with might and with main,
for the sinews are all standing out round his neck:
grey-haired, but his strength is the strength of a youth!
No distance away from the old fisherman
is a fair vineyard, loaded with deepening grapes.
A little boy sits on the stone wall to guard it:
about him two vixens—one roams the vine-rows,
making her pillage the pick of the grapes.
The other has crafty designs on his wallet,   50
plainly declaring he shall not escape her
until she's laid paws on his vittles for breakfast.
He is weaving a pretty cage of rushes
with asphodel stalks, to keep locusts in.
His mind is far from his wallet and vines,
so absorbed he is in the pleasure of weaving.
About the cup, in every direction,
the supple acanthus spreads its leaves:
an object to make a goatherd marvel,

*The Greekless reader's attention is at the outset drawn to the pronunciation
of the final syllable of feminine names ending in -e and masculine in -es. Thus
in the present poem: helichrýsē (1. 30), Aphrodítē, Anchísēs, Diomédēs; in
Idyll ɪɪ (ll. 15–17) Hécatē, Círcē, Perimédē; etc.

60   and strike your heart with amazement, too!
A goat and a massive round of curds
I paid the Calydnian boatman for it,
since when it has lain unsullied; it never
has touched my lips. It would please me much,
my friend, to make you a present of it,
in return for your singing your lovely anthem.
I am not making fun of you. Come, begin!
Pointless to keep music in store
till Hades bring all to blank oblivion.

THYRSIS

70   Begin the bucolic theme, kind Muses, begin!

I am Thyrsis of Etna: sweet is the voice of Thyrsis.
Where were you, nymphs, when Daphnis lay dying? Where
were you, nymphs? In Peneus' precincts or about Pindus?
You surely held not to the great River Anapus,
nor the summit of Etna, and holy waters of Acis.

        Begin the bucolic theme, kind Muses, begin!

At his dying the jackals and the wolves howled:
even the lion out of his covert wept!

        Begin the bucolic theme, kind Muses, begin!

80   At his feet, many cows and many bulls,
many calves and heifers lay mourning!

        Begin the bucolic theme, kind Muses, begin!

First came Hermes, from the mountain, saying, 'Daphnis,
Who makes you waste? For whom so much desire!'

        Begin the bucolic theme, kind Muses, begin!

Came cowherds, shepherds; goatherds came,
all questioning what ailed him. Came Priapus,
and said 'Poor Daphnis, why do you pine? Your girl
from spring to spring and every glade swift-foot—

    Begin the bucolic theme, kind Muses, begin!—   90

goes searching. You too star-crossed and too hapless are.
Cowherd were you called? More like a goatherd now!
The goatherd, when he sees the nannies ridden,
cries out his eyes he wasn't born a goat!

    Begin the bucolic theme, kind Muses, begin!

You, when you see how the girls are laughing, cry
your eyes out that you're not in the dance with them!'
He answered none of these, but bore his own,
his bitter love to the end determined on.

    Begin the bucolic theme: Muses, begin again!   100

Lastly came smiling Aphrodite—only
she hid her smile, pretending grief. She said:
'You boasted, Daphnis, you would give Eros a fall:
have you not been thrown yourself by the tormentor?'

    Begin the bucolic theme: Muses, begin again!

Then Daphnis spoke. 'Aphrodite, tyrant!
Cypris full of spite! Cypris enemy of man!
Already gloating that my every sun has set?
Eros shall rue Daphnis even in Hades!

    Begin the bucolic theme: Muses, begin again!   110

And haven't I heard of Cypris, that a cowherd . . . ?
Crawl off to Ida, then; crawl to Anchises!

Are there not oaks there? Galingale . . . ?
And the bees make a marvellous thrumming about the
  hives?

> Begin the bucolic theme: Muses, begin again!

Adonis, too; he is ripe, and he shepherds sheep,
and shoots the hare and hunts all manner of beast.

> Begin the bucolic theme: Muses, begin again!

Go, haste! Bid Diomedes stand again;
120 say "Fight with me; I am conquering Daphnis the herd!"

> Begin the bucolic theme: Muses, begin again!

O wolves! O jackals! O bears that lie in the mountains!
Farewell! No more will you see Daphnis the cowherd
in the coppices, the glades . . . no more! Farewell, Arethusa,
and streams that pour your waters clear down Thybris.

> Begin the bucolic theme: Muses, begin again!

This is I! This is Daphnis! Here I pastured by herds.
Daphnis, who here watered my bulls and heifers!

> Begin the bucolic theme: Muses, begin again!

130 Pan, Pan! Are you on the long ridge of Lycaon?
Do you range over mighty Mount Maenalus? Here, to the
  Isle
of Sicily! Leave the sheer peak of Helice; leave
Lycaonidas' tomb, that even the gods admire!

> Break the bucolic theme; break it off, Muses!

Here, my master: relieve me of this pipe of reeds,
caulked with wax—its breath so sweet, and trim
about the lip, with bands. . . . Already I
am Hades-bound: Eros pulls me down!

> Break the bucolic theme; break it off, Muses!

Now briars bear violets! Violets spring on thorns!   140
Junipers blossom with narcissus flowers,
and all things be confounded: pines grow pears!
Since Daphnis is dying, the hart may harry the hounds,
and mountain owls find tongue of nightingale!'

> Break the bucolic theme; break it off, Muses!

So much he spoke, and ceased. Then Aphrodite wished
to raise him up, but the thread of the Fates was all
spun out; so Daphnis came to the river; the flood hid
the man loved by the Muses, nor to the nymphs unpleasing.

> Break the bucolic theme; break it off, Muses!   150

Now give me the goat and the bowl, to milk her and pour
an offering to the Muses. Farewell a thousand times,
Muses! A sweeter song will I sing you hereafter.

GOATHERD
A mouth so sweet!—may it be filled with honey,
Thyrsis! Yes, honeycomb—and the sweet figs
of Aegilus be your food; you outsing the cicada!
There is your cup: notice how fresh it smells!
You would think it had been washed in the wells of the
    Hours.
Come here, Kissaitha! You milk her. Now, nannies all,
stop prancing about, or Billy'll be on your tails!   160

❦Idyll II

This Idyll, though it stands second in the editions of Theocritus, occupies a later position in some manuscripts, including the superior Ambrosian codex and the Antinoan papyrus, in which Idyll I is followed by our Idyll V. Idyll II is strikingly different from Idyll I, and their juxtaposition may have resulted from the superficial resemblance of the refrain construction. However, one underlying link between this Idyll and Idyll I is the theme most characteristic of Theocritus' outlook: the damaging effects of Eros on human happiness.

Here we meet no folk hero, but a very human girl, Simaetha. The name is that of a famous courtesan mentioned by Aristophanes, but our Simaetha is a suburbanite of the lower middle class, whose sights are set on the 'station above her', but whose respectable aim is marriage; so, apart from a suggestion of venality, the name's chief appropriateness may be its Doric form. Simaetha is out by the seashore at night with her maid, Thestylis, making preparations for a magic ritual to 'bind' her lover, Delphis, whose 'Eros has gone elsewhere'. Her magic centres on the turning of the iynx-wheel. *Iynx* (from which our word 'jinx' may be derived) is the wryneck, a bird whose peculiar mating habits may have suggested its use in love charms. Originally, a dead wryneck would have been splayed on the wheel, but Simaetha's wheel probably lacks this adornment. Other magic objects she uses are the rhombus (a metal plate on a string, which she whirls to 'produce' the giddiness of love) and various 'sympathetic' substances representing Delphis or parts of his body, which she burns (barley and laurel) or melts (wax) in token of 'firing' or 'melting' him with love, and in the former instances at least, with a secondary purpose of wreaking him bodily harm. The latter aim is irrational in view of the dominant motive displayed in the Iynx refrain, which is the regaining of Delphis; but the intermixture of crude vengefulness has psychological verisimilitude.

The sequence of stanzas in the incantatory section has been a matter of dispute among scholars because of discrepancies in the manuscript traditions. I have argued elsewhere, largely on dramatic and stylistic grounds, that the present order gives us the most psychologically convincing—and therefore most Theocritean—presentation of Simaetha.* In effect, the opening rites, with their part-vindictive aims, are followed by a ritual sacrifice of husks accompanied by a ritual conjuring of Artemis. The incantation is broken off when Simaetha hears dogs (already mentioned in the preparatory section as accompanying Hecate's visitations) howling in the city. She tells Thestylis to 'sound the brass'—a cymbal or gong, the purpose of which is to keep the infernal influences at a safe distance while she makes her suit to the goddess. It will already be clear from the references to dogs and to the infernal realms that Artemis, goddess of birth and wild nature, is one with Hecate, whose power is associated with death. The third of this pagan trinity is Selene, the Moon, who presides over the flux of life, and in whom, as patroness of the *éternel féminin*, Simaetha confides throughout the second half of the poem. Thus the composite Artemis-Hecate-Selene is the power of mortal life here below, and as such is occult, ambiguous, and dread. Being threefold, she haunts the 'three-ways' (intersections of three roads) and is approached by means of triple prayer and libation.

Following the uproar of dogs and gong, Simaetha's attention is arrested by the stillness of sea and winds. This stilling of the elements is a regular concomitant of Greco-Roman theophanies, but here it has particular dramatic point. Simaetha, gazing outwards, momentarily relieves her sinister and contorted emotions, and herself becomes conscious of the contrast. In this instant of clear vision, she touches our comprehension and pity

---

*Anna Rist, 'The Incantatory Sequence in Theocritus' Pharmaceutria', *Maia* 24(1975):103–11.

as she lays bare the nerve of her complaint: that she is left 'spoiled and no virgin, instead of a wife.'*

The formal action of her three libations, accompanied by a thrice-repeated prayer that Delphis may forget his current infatuation, reinforces this steadier mood. Throughout the stanza which follows, Simaetha is in a trancelike state through which her mind wanders in a train of associations drawn from mythology, from the Lethe-water of forgetfulness to the venereal plant hippomanes (the word seems to mean 'mare's drip') that grows in distant Arcadia and produces (erotic) mania in animals which browse it. Here, the thought of Delphis and her desire for him recurring, she starts from her reverie to renewed and redoubled (literally, for this stanza contains two acts, in contrast to the first two stanzas of the incantation, which contain one each) magic activity, aimed now unambiguously at his recovery. The goddess has been lost sight of; Theocritus, as well as we, may well regard her previous presence as self-induced in Simaetha's consciousness. The new series of incantations reaches a crescendo of frenzy as Simaetha cries out against Eros as the cause of her misery. She appears exhausted and doubtful, after all, of the efficacy of her magic, for she utters a final threat that she will bear (and somehow administer) to Delphis a deadly potion. The final injunction to Thestylis may refer to the ashes from the burning of the magic objects and be designed to bring them into physical contact with Delphis, at least symbolically, the 'bones' represented by his doorposts and the 'parts above' being presumably legs and pelvis.

The lurid scene of the spellbinding, lit as it is by fireglow and the flicker and spurt of flames, contrasts with the second half of the poem, when in a serene perspective of moonlight the melodrama appears dwindled to the proportions of the human breast, its seat. A glimpse of the participatory role of nature was given when Simaetha, in the full spate of her obsession, became briefly aware of the silence of sea and winds. And as, at the end of her

---

*Here and elsewhere I have given a prose rendering of the Greek, which the reader may compare with the verse translation.

monologue, she bids the horses of the Moon fare onward on their appointed course, we realize that the powers to which she has been appealing are unmoved by the disorders of human passion. It is man who has to conform himself to their silence and their order, if he can, and the tranquil ending suggests that in her communing Simaetha has obtained a measure of peace.

Indeed, Theocritus sometimes seems to hesitate between viewing the Eros affliction as a wanton folly of man or as a disease which must be borne or cured by such means as the individual may find (cf. Idylls XI and XIV)—the dilemma of Idyll XXX, where he remonstrates with himself on his infatuation. Simaetha, in fact, behaves very much like the contemporary victims of Eros recorded in the pages of popular women's magazines, and the dispassionate may wonder if she is a victim to the sense of being victimized. Having engineered the original debacle, she now persists in casting herself in the romantic role, setting out to bemoan her lot, recalling every circumstance to work on her emotions and excite her vengeance. Her trite old story—the girl who has been 'bowled over', has 'offered herself on a plate', has been 'jilted'—she dramatizes, clothing its culmination in the language of religion, 'the great rite' about which she will not 'babble' being a verbal reference to the injunction to silence at the Eleusinian and other Mysteries. This self-aggrandizement, while it is made possible by a religious appreciation of the cosmic mystery of sex, also lends an endearing realism and even humour to the presentation of Simaetha, who to us must be a familiar enough figure—the anonymous child of the city (Cos, or perhaps Alexandria) who experiences the need to assert her importance in the scheme of things.

The people among whom Simaetha lives are tantalizingly sketched by her passing references: the girl Anaxo, who has the distinction of a part in religious processions; the Thracian nurse next door, agog for every new spectacle; Clearista, on whose wardrobe Simaetha draws, we may suppose by a mutual arrangement; Delphis and Eudamippus, a pair of vain and well-heeled young 'blades' who loaf around the wrestling school between bouts and spend their evenings in carousing and erotic

escapades; the local gossip who can be relied on to come run-
ning with her latest news and views straight to those whom
they may concern; her daughter who earns pin money by play-
ing background music on the flute when Simaetha entertains
Delphis—a touch of sophistication Simaetha would not deny
herself. The gently satiric strokes with which these personages
and Simaetha herself are presented in all their dear vulgarity
connect this poem with the mimes, Idylls XIV and XV.

We may further notice the impartial realism with which Theo-
critus treats men and women alike. True, his women may come,
in one sense, less well out of the comparison; they are hardly
forces to be reckoned with, as are the women of his great pre-
decessors in realism, Aristophanes and Euripides. Perhaps Theo-
critus was too much of a realist to portray heroic women in his
day and age, though he might flatter the memory of a great
lady, Berenice (as a great lord, Ptolemy) for politic reasons. So
the legendary mother of Heracles is introduced in homely wise,
putting her babies to bed and rousing her husband in the night
with agelong verisimilitude, despite a veneer of heroic conven-
tion. Even Helen of Troy, in a formal epithalamium, is seen
chiefly as a Spartan girl preeminent among her comrades, and is
praised for her domestic skills. In Simaetha, as in Praxinoa and
Gorgo of Idyll XV, Theocritus accords women the tribute of
being human characters and intrinsically interesting. In Simae-
tha, moreover, he exposes and inveighs against the Eros idolatry
to which our own age is as prone as any, and of which he him-
self well knew the deception and frustration, even as it capti-
vated him through the beauty of boys (see Idyll XXX). Though
Plato and the Platonic tradition before and after him taught that
the psychic drive of Eros might, by a rational asceticism, be
directed onto an ultimately satisfying, self-transcending object,
Theocritus found, it seems, no solution but submission.

The Spellbinders

(Simaetha and her maid)

Where are the laurels? Bring them me, Thestylis. Where
    are the philtres?
Wreathe crimson wool, the choicest, round the bowl;
charms I'll bind on the man, my lover and my bane!
Twelve days I've waited and the brute has not come
    near me,
and whether I'm dead or alive he hasn't cared to discover;
not so much as a knock at the door, so monstrous is he!
So Eros has gone and taken his fickle fancy elsewhere!
Aphrodite too! Tomorrow I'll to Timaegetus' palaestra,
to let him know to his face how ill he uses me;
but first, today, I'll bind him fast with my fire-sorcery.   10
Shine clear, Moon: low, in your hushed ears,
shall my spells be sung, goddess, and to her, the earthbound
Hecate, before whom the dog-pack cowers
when she comes among the tombs for the black blood of
    corpses.
Hail, dread Hecate! Attend us to the close,
working direr magic than any Circe worked;
than any of Medeia, or blonde-haired Perimede.

    Bird-wheel, turn, and hale him home, my man!

First your barley chars on the fire: scatter it on,
Thestylis! Scared, are you, like a bird, out of your wits?   20
What, are you out to make a fool of me, wretch—you too?
Scatter the barley and say, 'I am scattering Delphis' bones.'

    Bird-wheel, turn, and hale him home, my man!

Delphis has made me smart, so I make laurel blaze,
and turn the blaze on Delphis. As it catches fire and crackles,

and all at once is gone, not even ash to see—
so may the flesh of Delphis fall away in flame!

> Bird-wheel, turn, and hale him home, my man!

Now I'll fire the husks. You, Artemis, move
30   the iron gates of hell, or any stronger bar!
Thestylis, all the dogs in the city give us tongue:
the goddess, at the three ways! Quickly, clash the brass!

> Bird-wheel, turn, and hale him home, my man!

Behold! The sea is silent and silent are the winds;
but not stilled the tempest raging in my breast!
My whole being burns to be avenged on him
who has cast me no wife's, but a spoiled virgin's lot.

> Bird-wheel, turn, and hale him home, my man!

I pour the three libations, and three times, mistress, cry:
40   Whether another woman lies beside him, or a man,
may he of Lethe have as much as once, in Naxos,
Theseus took, they say, to forget fair Ariadne.

> Bird-wheel, turn, and hale him home, my man!

In Arcady there grows a plant, hippomanes; it maddens
all the colts on the mountainsides, with the fleet mares.
Thus might I see Delphis, and he bolt here home,
like a mad thing loosed from the slippery palaestra.

> Bird-Wheel turn, and hale him home, my man!

As I wax waste by the power of the fire god, so
50   straightway, by Eros' power, may Myndian Delphis waste;
and as this bronze rhombus spins Aphrodite's dance,
so may that same dance spin Delphis to our doors.

Bird-wheel, turn, and hale him home, my man!

This fringe of his cloak has Delphis lost in forfeit!
I'll tear it like a beast, and throw it on the fire.
Aiai, tormenting Eros! Why have you clamped on my veins
like a marsh leech, and drained the dark blood out?

Bird-wheel, turn, and hale him home, my man!

Tomorrow I'll pound a lizard and bear you the noxious
    brew;
now—Thestylis, take these preparations. While it is night,   60
smear them on his door, the parts above the jambs,
and whisper these words the while, 'I smear Delphis' bones.'

Bird-wheel turn, and hale him home, my man!

Now that I am alone, how to begin to tell
my woeful love story? Who brought this curse on me?
It all happened when Euboulus' daughter, Anaxo, was
    going
as basket bearer to Artemis' grove; they were staging a
    procession—
leading all kinds of animals round, among them a lioness.

Tell, how fell Eros on me, Lady Moon!

And Theumarida, the Thracian nurse—God rest her soul!   70
She lived next door—she begged us almost on her knees
to be spectators at the show, and I, misguided that I was!
tagged along with her, trailing my best linen dress,
topped off with a wrap I borrowed from Clearista.

Tell, how fell Eros on me, Lady Moon!

Hardly half way along the road—about at Lycon's—
I saw Delphis: he was walking with Eudamippus.
Their beards were more golden than curling honeysuckle,

and their chests had such a sheen—brighter than you,
   Moon,—
for they were fresh returned from the genteel toil of the
80   gym.

     Tell, how fell Eros on me, Lady Moon!

The moment my eyes lit on them, madness lit on me,
and fire was laid to my heart, poor wretch that I am!
My looks were a faded flower; I took no more note of
   processions,
and I know not how I got home; a burning fever was
   shaking me,
and I lay in my bed for all of ten days and nights.

     Tell, how fell Eros on me, Lady Moon!

And my flesh, more often than not, was the colour
   of boxwood,
and every last hair fell out of my head; I was reduced
90   to skin and bone. What dame's establishment did I not visit?
Did I omit the house of a single crone that crooned?
But I found no cure, and time went running on to the
   close.

     Tell, how fell Eros on me, Lady Moon!

So I told the whole truth to my slave. I said, 'Thestylis,
listen, you must find me some cure for this disease;
it's killing me: my poor soul's all possessed by the Myndian.
So go and keep a lookout near Timaegetus' palaestra,
for that's his favourite haunt; that's where he suns himself.

     Tell, how fell Eros on me, Lady Moon!

And when you learn that he's alone, beckon to him, and
100   say—

discreetly, mind—"Simaetha calls you," and lead him here.'
No sooner said—she was gone, and returned to the house
   with Delphis,
the sheen on his skin! And I, as soon as I was aware,
by the light footfall, it was he crossing the threshold—

      Tell, how fell Eros on me, Lady Moon!

I froze, through and through, to the bone, colder than
   snow,
and the sweat ran from my forehead, more like a heavy
   dew.
I couldn't utter a word, not so much as the broken word
children whimper in sleep to their mother. My once fresh
complexion became like a wax doll, exactly!   110

      Tell, how fell Eros on me, Lady Moon!

After a glance, the unnatural man stared at the floor,
and sat on the bed and made me a speech: 'Simaetha,
   I swear
you've outstripped me by no more than the edge I had on
   the fair
Philinus lately in the race! There was not *that* between
your sending for me to your home here, and my coming
   myself.

      Tell, how fell Eros on me, Lady Moon!

I was about to come—in fact, this very night;
I swear it by sweet Eros—with two or three friends to
   back me,
and all got up—Dionysus' apples hidden in my cloak,   120
and on my head a sprig of Heracles' own tree,
the white poplar, wound round with a crimson ribbon.

      Tell, how fell Eros on me, Lady Moon!

And if you had opened to me, it would have been
    becoming,
for I'm thought handsome and athletic as any of the boys.
I'd have slept in peace if I'd only kissed your pretty mouth.
But if you'd turned me away and barred your door, against
    you
axes and torches were ready to advance on every side.

      Tell, how fell Eros on me, Lady Moon!

130   Now first I declared my debt to Cypris and, madam, you
are second only to Cypris, for you hauled me out of the
    fire
when you sent for me here to your residence, already half
consumed as I was—and Eros' blaze can surely scorch
fiercer than the glare of Liparos, Vulcan's mountain;

      Tell, how fell Eros on me, Lady Moon!

and with his wicked ravings he hounds virgins, even,
from their chambers—even brides to leave their husbands'
    beds
still warm.' These were his words and—gullible me!—
I took his hand and lay back on the yielding bed.
140   Soon skin warmed to skin, and our faces grew
hotter than before; we exchanged thrilling whispers.
Not to detain you with babble of intimate matters, Moon,
the great rite was performed, and we both attained our end.
He found no fault with me, nor I with him, till yesterday.
But as soon as Dawn's horses went racing up the sky
    today,
bearing her all rosy from Ocean's bed, the mother
of Melixo and Philista—she who played the flute for us—
came with the latest, and told me Delphis, if you please,
is in love! Whether it was a woman this time, or a man,
150   she didn't rightly know, but she knew he kept on toasting
Eros in potent cups, and finally rushed out shouting

that he'd festoon his object's doors with the garlands he
   was wearing.
That was my neighbour's story, and she would tell what
   she knew.
Besides, he used to visit me three or four times a day
and often he left his flagon,* as he called it, in my keeping.
Today's the twelfth that I've not set eyes on him. What can
   that mean,
but that he's taking his pleasure elsewhere, and I'm
   forgotten! Well,
for today I'll bind him with spells, but if he should cross
   me still,
by all the Fates, I swear, it's the gates of hell he shall
   hammer on:
such unholy elixirs—I don't mind telling you, Mistress—   160
as I've stored in my coffer for him, that I had from a gypsy.
Now, Lady, fare you well; your foals fare on to the ocean.
As for me, I will bear my yearning—as I must bear it.
Farewell, Moon, on your gleaming throne; attendant stars,
revolving in the train of tranquil Night, fare well.

*The flask containing the oil Greek athletes used to anoint themselves. This
custom gives part of its sense to the expression 'slippery palaestra' (wrestling
school) above, 1. 47. Simaetha uses the dialect word she has heard from
Delphis.

ꙮ Idyll III

This Idyll might be characterized as an essay in the grotesque, a style found comparably in Damoetas' song in Idyll VI, and also in Idyll V, but there at a seemingly more realistic level. Here, in the amorous poet-goatherd, the grotesque takes on the tinge of fantasy which was to make it for later ages so captivating a Hellenistic motif, epitomized in the visual arts by the satyr figures, those demons of the Arcadian landscape, human in their art and goatish in their instincts, to whom Theocritus' goatherds in particular bear affinity. In Idyll VII, Theocritus will perfect his modelling of the grotesque-fantastic in the figure of Lycidas, in comparison with whom the present poet-goatherd is a mere rhymster and buffoon. From our consideration of the goatherd Battus in the introduction to Idyll IV will emerge yet profounder implications of this Theocritean figure.

We come upon the present specimen of the genre as he prepares to leave his herd in charge of one Tityrus (quite possibly the leading goat; the name at least has that sense in the Spartan dialect, though it could also be a man's name derived from his occupation—as Virgil, in his first Eclogue, takes it to be) and perform the *kōmos*, or serenade, outside his mistress's dwelling.*
His abrupt opening announcement to this effect is meant to indicate his boorish character, and the grotesque is already apparent in the notion of a low-class bumpkin aping a custom of polite city society, whereby late revellers made their way to their mistress's house to demand admittance, first with music and song and entreaty and, that failing, with assaults on the doors (cf. Idyll II), or alternatively leaving the suitor to lie at the door all night to

---

*The quasi-technical word *paraclausithuron* ('a song at closed doors') is used elsewhere in the present work. In literature the term is first found in Plutarch's *Amatorius*.

impress on the lady the earnestness of his suit—as does our goat-
herd, with ludicrous effect, at the end of the present poem. The
full absurdity of the situation stands out when we learn that
Amaryllis' dwelling is a cave and the only barrier to his entry a
curtain of foliage. It seems that the pangs of libidinousness (only
thinly veiled by the conventional apparatus of Greek suitors,
music and garlands) are less potent in him than his preoccupation
with gentility or, it may be, his respect for his 'black-browed
nymph'. It is typical of Theocritus' humanity that he arouses a
degree of sympathy even for this uncouth figure, as he reveals the
feelings of inferiority and rejection which, we may suppose, serve
to keep the goatherd submissive to her. He is hypersensitive, as
befits a poet, however lowly and ignorant (which his supersti-
tions mark him as being). Amaryllis, it transpires, has admitted
him in the past, and his fall from favour leads him to doubt his
physical attractiveness at close quarters, and this incidentally
adds to the satyr picture we are forming of him. We may even
suspect—knowing that nymphs are seldom so squeamish—that
it is his very self-distrust and holding back from the assault sym-
bolically suggested by the cave mouth with its screen of ivy and
fern that but confirms him in Amaryllis' disdain—a touch of
the insight into feminine psychology which Theocritus displays
with broader effects in Idylls II and xv.

Following the brief introductory scene-setting, the bulk of the
poem consists of the monody in which the goatherd gives vent,
for the benefit of his mistress and the audience, to the successive
turns of his writhings and grovellings. He entreats, deprecates,
cajoles, wanders into sexual fantasy, girds at Eros, then at Ama-
ryllis, childishly threatens destruction, first of his garlands, then
of himself. His despair, though ludicrous, is a real enough force
upon him, though Theocritus may appear to suggest that his
situation, as is the case of Simaetha, is a malign deception of
Eros or, subjectively, manufactured to fill some perverse need
for self-assertion. In the end the goatherd is reduced to the bar-
ren support of superstition, but he pulls himself together suffi-
ciently to sing a formal ode, which we may presume he has
composed in advance for the occasion, on the successful suits of

various legendary lovers. His mythological erudition here is as improbable as his whole situation and follows particularly incongruously on his rustic superstitions. The suggestion again is that he is emulating city culture. His examples are handpicked: Hippomenes, who enticed the Amazon Hippolyta with golden apples, is suggested by the goatherd's love token; Bias' eligibility as a suitor rested on the possession of herds, and he is himself a herdsman; Adonis and Endymion were famous for the beauty that he lacks and longs for. This, however, makes their choice ill-considered: in his wilful romanticizing of his situation the goatherd overlooks the fact that he must be the loser in the comparison. Moreover, the ending of their stories is less than happy, as is also the case with Iasion, who met his death on account of the love of Demeter. Partly he realizes this, for he alludes to the death of Adonis, killed by Artemis after he became the lover of Aphrodite, and to the perpetual sleep of Endymion, loved by the Moon. He is suggesting that no price is too high to pay for the embrace of the beloved. Partly he is too naive to recognize the ill portent, being more struck with the opportunity for flattering Amaryllis which the comparisons afford.

Still meeting with no response, he makes, like the rejected Cyclops in Idyll XI, a childish bid for sympathy: his head is aching, but what does she care! Finally he prostrates himself on the ground before her cave, and announces a 'lie-in'—in the *kōmos* convention a regular alternative to battering down the door. With him it is rather a gesture of petulance, as his words show, and we are left sceptical as to how long his agitation will allow him to remain quiescent.

The Goatherd's Serenade

I go to serenade my Amaryllis.
My goats are grazing on the mountainside,
Tityrus in charge. Tityrus, darling,
graze the goats, then drive them to the spring.
Watch the Libyan, Mustard, or he'll butt you.

Amaryllis, my pretty, why don't you peek out
and invite me into your cave these days?
Am I not your sweetheart? Do you hate me?

Could it be that at close quarters,
girl, you find me snub-nosed,   10
or stub-bearded? You'll make me go swing!

Here—I've brought your apples, ten,
picked from the spot you told me yourself.
Tomorrow I'll go to fetch you more.

Look at me, won't you—stricken with this love-ache!
How gladly I'd change with that bumbling bee,
I'd have the entrée then to your cave—
zoom through your ivy and fern-leaf screen!

Now I know Eros—a thug of a god!
Didn't he suck the dug of a lioness,   20
bred in the backwoods? See how he licks me;
the flame sears right to the bone!

And you, with your witching glances, you're made
of stone! Witch, with the black brows,
embrace me, your goatherd! Let me kiss you!
There's pleasure enough in only kissing.

In a moment you'll make me tear this garland
in shreds—and I was bringing it for you,

Amaryllis! Dear one! It's of ivy,
30   twined with buds and scented celery.

Alas, poor devil that I am!
This is unbearable. Won't you hear me?

I'll take off my cloak and jump in the sea
from the point where Olpis the fisherman keeps
a watch for tunny. Either I'll drown,
or at least your vanity will be tickled.

I knew it the other day; I was trying
whether you loved me, but at the smack,
the far-love petal, instead of clinging,
40   wilted away on my forearm, useless.

And Agraeo, she read my fortune aright,
with her sieve; she was gathering grasses one day
and came up alongside. 'She you have staked
your heart on', she said, 'makes no account of it.'

And besides, I've a grey she-goat with twins
I was keeping for you, but that sallow piece,
Memnon's scivvy, keeps begging me for it,
and shall have it, since you put on these airs.

My right eye's twitching. Am I to see her?
50   I'll step aside, under this pine tree,
and sing. It may be she'll spare me a glance.
She's not made of flint entirely, is she?

(sings)
Hippomenes, when he wished to wed
a maid, took apples in his hand
and ran a race. When Atalanta
saw him, how she lost her head!
Plumb into Eros took the leap!

To Pylos Seer Melampus from the land
of Othrys drove a herd: the charms
of the mother of Alphesiboea the Wise   60
came to rest in Bias' arms.

And on the mountains, herding sheep,
did not Adonis bring to the crest
of madness Cytherea? Even dead,
she puts him not away from her breast.

Even Endymion, who lies
under the unreverting sleep,
is enviable, lady, in my eyes.
Even Iasion, who won
joys to the uninitiate not known.   70

My head is aching, but what do you care!
I'll sing no more, but lie where I have fallen.
The wolves shall eat me. Let that stick
in your throat, and taste as sweet as honey!

❧Idyll IV

This interlude achieves an effect of simplicity and naturalism not matched elsewhere in Theocritus' poems. It dispenses with the device of song within song (although an opening for this is provided at ll. 32ff.) and uses plain and at times racy dialogue. Its setting immediately suggests comparison with Idyll I, with which it shares the dramatic locality of Croton in southern Italy and also the name of Philondas, who receives mention in both as a man of property. By comparison, Idyll V, while using vulgarisms less picturesquely, maintains a greater formalism of tone and scene.

Dramatic interest in Idyll IV arises largely from the portrayal of Battus, to whom Corydon serves as a foil. Since the name Battus means 'Stammerer', we are soon struck by a paradox in his presentation, for he possesses an agile mind and tongue, whereas Corydon is literal-minded and platitudinous. Corydon means 'Lark', so that Theocritus seems to be dropping a strong hint that men are not necessarily as they appear to be. (The melodious name of Corydon was in fact seized on by countless generations of pastoral poets who had long shed their founder's irony, and bestowed upon a literary pedigree of 'rustics' far more 'idyllic' than their original.) The paradox of Battus' character is reinforced at line 40, where we are given to understand, for the first and only time, that he is a goatherd, albeit out of his own haunts and, it appears, without his flock. Now goatherds are conventionally, for the Greeks, the lowliest of rustics, men remarkable mainly for their crudeness of clay—a character they share with their animals. Shepherds rank above them and cowherds stand at the head of the pecking order. Corydon is, at least temporarily, classed with the latter. Clearly Idyll IV is less straightforward than at first sight it seems to be.

Moreover, on closer consideration, what looks like a random conversation turns out to be contrived so as to direct the sequence of topics round a theme, that of the kinship of man and beast*—an area probably more foreign to the outlook of the modern reader than to Theocritus' contemporaries, let alone his bucolic characters. We find that each cow and bull has its preferred diet, and that the animals cannot be expected to abide the substitution of a strange herdsman, however solicitous for their welfare. Their thinness, arising from 'lovesickness', reminds us of Simaetha in Idyll II and of Aeschinas in Idyll XIV.

In a related vein—that of the likeness of tender feeling for both humans and animals—is Battus' odd comment called forth by the mention of the dead Amaryllis: 'dear to me as my she-goats'. The quality of his feeling is shown both in his momentary dejection, on which Corydon comments, and in his choice of the word 'quenched', which is more naturally used of a flame, and so of the flame of Eros, than of a life. The preceding thumbnail sketch of Aegon's prank with the bull—symbol of masculine strength and eroticism—already suggests that he has been Battus' competitor in love, and also gives us a glimpse of Amaryllis, a creature of flesh and blood among a group of farm women (she is in no way to be identified with the shadowy nymph of Idyll III).

Keeping in mind Battus' comparison of his love for Amaryllis with his feelings towards his she-goats—and also the traditionally amorous propensities of goatherds (typified in Priapus' crudely phrased remarks to Daphnis in Idyll I)—we may interpret his subsequent 'gawping after' a heifer in an erotic, or quasi-erotic sense, symbolized, as has been observed, by the thorn which at that moment pierces his foot and recalls the dart of Eros.† Perhaps we should rather see this as the symbolism the incident contains for Battus himself, in keeping with his imaginative character, and in particular implied in his poetic remark

*Here I follow, in the main, Gilbert W. Lawall, 'Theocritus' Fourth Idyll: Animal Loves and Human Loves', *Rivista di filologia e di istruzione classica* 94 (1966):42–50.
†By Lawall, *ibid*.

about the 'little wound' which 'masters a man of my size'.
However, the thorn is also a real thorn—the prosaic Corydon
points out that the hillside is covered with them—and at a more
immediate level of symbolism it is a reminder of the harshness
and contrariness of life which lets the longing of man or beast
go unsatisfied. Furthermore the thorn serves as the occasion of
the topics that follow: Battus' gazing at the heifer and the 'old
lecher' of the conclusion.

In this last turn that Battus gives to the dialogue, we sense
dramatically the painfulness of his feelings in his abrupt with-
drawal from preoccupation with them. His acute susceptibility
has been stirred by the mention of Amaryllis, by the spectacle
of the heifer, to which he attributes a comparable loss and long-
ing, and generally, we may assume, by the poignancy of old
acquaintance and haunts revisited. In Aegon's father, whose
advanced age underscores his lasciviousness, he and we are pre-
sented by contrast with the elemental unsublimated libido, in
man the substrate of Eros in all his guises. In this poem it is illu-
strated only in man and nowhere in beast, whereas at the close
of Idyll v the antics of the billy goat provide a parting comment
on the smouldering passions of the protagonists. In that Idyll,
too, we shall find that the goatherd, Comatas—warped old man
though he be—is an abler poet and a nimbler wit than the
shepherd, Lacon. We begin to appreciate why the figure of man
the poet, the maker (*poiētēs*), is appropriately seen emerging
from this character role. In Idyll vii—as it were the culmination
of a goatherd trilogy—we shall find the goatherd figure whose
libido is sublimated into poetry in full flower in Lycidas, and we
shall have more to say in the introduction to that Idyll about the
latter's relation to Theocritus the poet.

Thus it is plain that Battus, too, relates in some way to Theo-
critus, though, as I have shown, it is rather through the motif of
the goatherd-poet (which culminates in Lycidas) than by a direct
equivalence, for which it is hard to find warrant in Idyll iv itself.
There we find, it is true, one direct suggestion of a poetic role
for Battus in the mention of 'the pipes that once I fashioned', in
line 29. On the surface, this is slight enough in view of the con-

ventional association between piping and herding; however, the rather gratuitous way in which the mention of pipes is introduced may invite us to treat them with special attention, and if we are to take Battus as 'in fact' a townsman posing as a rustic, we must allow them a particular significance as pointing to his character as poet *and hence* as a rightful bucolic and herdsman.

Striking too is the fact that in Idyll VII the learner-poet, to be identified in some way with Theocritus, bears a name comparable to that of Battus in its paradoxically prosaic connotation. Further, we shall find him, Simichidas, wearing 'citified boots' inappropriate to a rustic, while in the present poem Battus' lack of any footwear—for which he is reproved by the unquestionably authentic Corydon—betrays him as no true countryman,* but rather, I would suggest, as one overdoing a role. As culminating evidence, we may point to his witty comments throughout, and in particular to the political jibe at lines 21–23, as strongly suggesting the sophistication of the cultured city-dweller. And in a more general way we may remark that Battus' poetic susceptibility and accompanying proneness to pain—the inner 'wound' symbolized for him by the thorn—may well remind us of the suffering Theocritus who complains in his own persona in Idyll XXX.

*This was observed by J. van Sickle and others before S. Lattimore suggested the identification of Battus with Theocritus. See the articles listed at Idyll IV in the Bibliography.

Battus

(Battus and Corydon)

BATTUS
Corydon, tell me, who owns those cattle? Is it Philondas?

CORYDON
No, Aegon; he's handed them over to me to graze.

BATTUS
Do you perhaps milk them all in the evenings, on the
  quiet?

CORYDON
The old 'un puts the calves to suck, and keeps his eye on me.

BATTUS
And whither, pray, has himself, our cowherd, vanished
  away?

CORYDON
You've not heard? Milon went and took him off to
  Olympia.

BATTUS
Olympia! Since when have his sights been set on the ring?

CORYDON
Why, they say he's a match for Heracles in might and
  muscle.

BATTUS
My mother used to compare me with Pollux—to his
  disadvantage!

CORYDON
Anyway, he's gone: with a pickaxe and twenty sheep
   from the flock.   10

BATTUS
Milon can use his persuasion on the wolves too, to run
   riot!

CORYDON
These heifers certainly miss him. That's why they never
   stop lowing.

BATTUS
Poor beasts that they are! They've not done too well for a
   herdsman.

CORYDON
Poor beasts is right! They don't even fancy food these
   days.

BATTUS
Just look at that heifer! Nothing but skin and bones!
You don't feed her on dewdrops, do you, like a cicada?

CORYDON
So help me, no! Sometimes I pasture her on the Aesarus,
and I give her a fine bale of soft hay. Other times,
she frisks in the cool shade around Latymnus way.

BATTUS
That bull, the ruddy one, 's not got much substance either.   20
Lampriadas' boys ought to get one like him,
when the demesmen are offering their sacrifices to Hera.
That's a deme doesn't exactly do honour to its gods!

CORYDON

But I swear he's driven to the river flats, and Physcus'
    lands,
and over to the Neaethus, where there's everything
    growing that's good:
restharrow, fleabane, scented balm. . . .

BATTUS

Alas, o wretched Aegon! Your herds will go down
    to Hades!
And all because you fell for a victor's blighted crown!
The pipes that once I fashioned are spotted now with
    mildew. . . .

CORYDON

Not at all! No, by the nymphs! For when he went off to
30   Olympia,
he left them me as a gift. I am something of a musician:
I can strike up Glauce's songs, and Pyrrho's—I'm good at
    those—
and sing the 'Praises of Croton'—'Fairest of towns is
    Zacynthus',
and the other bit, 'the Lacinian temple toward the dawn'—
that's where Basher Aegon put down eighty cakes,
single-handed! And where he pulled the bull by the hoof
off the mountainside, and presented it to Amaryllis.
Didn't the women let out a yell—and didn't he laugh!

BATTUS

Dear Amaryllis! The only girl we shall not forget
dead though you be! Dear to me as my she-goats,
40   and yet—snuffed out! An accursèd fate is mine!

CORYDON

Cheer up, Battus, old man! Things may be better
    tomorrow.
While there's life there's hope, and only the dead are done
    for.

Zeus sends blue skies sometimes, and sometimes he sends
    rain. . . .

BATTUS
I'm greatly cheered! Here, chase those calves up the hill:
they're gnawing the olive shoots, the devils!

CORYDON
      Get along, Shiner!
Get along, Ripple! Get up that hill! D'you hear me? By
    Pan!
I'll come and be your death if you don't get out of it! Look
how that one's stealing back! I need a stout stick to take to
    you!

BATTUS
For God's sake, Corydon, help! A thorn's just stuck in me
    —here,
under the ankle. The ground's thick with brambles. Hang   50
the heifer! It was gawping at her I got spiked. Do you
    see it?

CORYDON
There, there! I've got it with my nails—and here's itself.

BATTUS
Such a little wound, and it masters a man of my size!

CORYDON
You shouldn't go barefoot when you're out on the hillside,
    Battus;
this whole hillside's covered with thorns and brambles,
    you know.

BATTUS
Here, Corydon, tell me: Is the old man still screwing
that black-browed baby he used to be so hot on?

Idyll IV

CORYDON
More than ever, brother! I came upon him myself,
the other day, right by the sheepfold—caught on the job!

BATTUS
60 Bravo, old lecher! Now, there's a breed for you!
They nigh outmatch the satyrs and the scrawny-shanked
    Pans!

⚜ Idyll V

Comatas, a goatherd and slave of Eumaras, encounters Lacon, a shepherd and slave of Sibyrtas.* The locality is Thurii, a neighbouring town to Croton in southern Italy, which had formerly been called Sybaris from a previous foundation in the area. It seems from this poem that the inhabitants, or some of them, were still known as Sybarites—or there may have been still an adjoining town or village of Sybaris; or perhaps the lake mentioned at the end of the poem served to keep the name alive. At all events, Eumaras is referred to as 'the Sybarite', and Comatas so refers to Lacon, in irony probably, since a slave could not strictly be a citizen. It seems that Lacon puts on airs to the older Comatas; his occupation already gives him more status than the latter's, and he refers to himself formally, though absurdly, by a 'patronymic' derived from his mother's name, thereby suggesting that he is a home-born slave, whereas Comatas, it may be presumed, has been purchased and is of unknown origin. Lacon hopes that Morson will assume his flock is his own, and is annoyed when Comatas makes a point of naming the owner.

Their servile status is underscored, no doubt to account for the coarseness of their attitudes and speech, which contrast with the polite encounters of Idylls I, VI, and VII and even with the naturalistic exchanges of Idyll IV. The fact that the sullen and lewd Comatas bears the same name as the rustic hero in Lycidas' song in Idyll VII only underlines his uncouthness and adds to the contrast. The Greeks commonly viewed slavery as affecting the souls of men, actually diminishing their human and moral worth. Society's dependence for its maintenance and cultural

*If not legally slaves (though l. 119 would suggest that Comatas is), they are serfs, dependent on their masters for their living.

advance on the enslavement of many tended to impede any questioning of the practice on ethical grounds, though its generally deleterious effect on human character was an accurate enough psychological observation frequently found in writers from Homer on.

In contrast to the courteous invitations of Idylls I and VII, and the easy accord of VI, this dialogue, from the opening accusations of theft and all through the squabble over the stakes and the site for the singing contest, consists of deliberate provocation by both parties. For a while the reader may be uncertain whether they are really angry or whether their coarse raillery is but uncouth manners and basically friendly, but by most standards it appears to bite deeper than this, and it is hard to overlook the malice in such lines as Comatas' taunt at lines 41–42 and Lacon's rejoinder. When Comatas, 'merely telling the truth', takes pains to prevent Lacon's posing to Morson as owner of his flock, and Lacon shortly afterwards reminds Comatas of the beating he once received from his master, we may at most conclude that previously they have been themselves attempting to mask their hostile feelings—an interpretation which would align the poem with others in which Theocritus displays comparable dramatic subtlety. Moreover, the root of their ambivalence has by now been exposed, and we understand why their hostility takes a different form in each, Comatas becoming aggressive and Lacon affecting indifference. In the past, the elder Comatas has initiated the boy Lacon homosexually—'teaching' for which he claims 'gratitude'. His relish in the memory is sufficient reason for Lacon's evasion of it.

Comatas, from his opening gambit, casts himself as the aggrieved party, which may account for why he is treated as the challenger and opens the contest (cf. Idyll VI), although it is Lacon who first invites the match. The contest takes the form of alternating couplets, in which the respondent (Lacon) is required to pick up and vary themes stated by the challenger (Comatas). The effect is of a close cut-and-thrust, and contrasts with the singing matches of Idylls VI and VII, where each of the participants offers an extended passage of song and the competitors are basically in harmony, the singing match providing a means of fraternization among rustic poets (VI) or their imitators (VII). Comatas and Lacon are bitterly at variance, and the main aim of their contest, as they are at pains to draw to the attention of the judge, Morson, is to 'gall' each other. This must be borne in mind in assessing Morson's decision in favour of Comatas. Critics who have failed to find the latter's verse notably superior have found the award arbitrary or fallen back on the suggestion that it turns on the musical performance, and that the reader is to take it on trust. This seems inadequate. Gow points out that some judgment is necessary. Moreover, Theocritus cannot be expected to present us with a series of defective verses.

But is there in fact no indication of the rationale for the judgment in the purely literary material before us? I suggest that Comatas comes off the better in aiming verbal thrusts at his opponent, and this because of his greater inventiveness in insult. Granted that Lacon's scope is reduced by the need to cap Comatas' couplets, he rises inadequately to the challenge, and his ripostes have a tendency to fall flat. Some simply profess superiority, while others are mere imitations of Comatas', with no added piquancy. Comatas, meanwhile, leaps from insinuation to insinuation. He begins with fairly conventional flyting, boasting of the patronage of the Muses, and of fortune in wealth and in love, decries Lacon's comparisons in an elegantly turned conceit which Lacon imitates too labouredly, and proceeds to describe with imaginative and hyperbolic touches the gifts he is keeping for his girl: a bird and a work of art. Lacon vies with rather pragmatic gifts for his boy-love: a cloak and a hunting dog. Between the descriptions of the two pairs of gifts is a realistic break of two couplets directed at the animals, which are straying, and also affording Comatas time for invention.

The exchanges on the objects of their affections have a strong dramatic undercurrent, for Comatas displays interest only in women and Lacon only in boys. Both are professing repudiation of their former sexual connection, and while Lacon may merely be intimating that the 'humpbacked' Comatas is too old and too little choice to interest him now, Comatas at least may be suspected of trying to excite Lacon's jealousy and regain his power over him. The sexual innuendos are continued in the exchange about 'shagtailed foxes' and 'beetles which blight the figs'— which last incites Comatas to a directness which Lacon parries, but with an emphasis which gives a new cue to his resourceful adversary, who claims to have piqued him, and invites Morson to take due precaution against the evil eye! Lacon's reply is mere imitation, asserting that he too has 'chafed' Comatas and proposing another and less striking remedy. Comatas thereafter tries a couple of conventional conceits, which Lacon varies well enough, and returns to the love theme, with its more provocative undertones. The twist he gives his couplet, casting himself this time as the slighted lover, and the colour it gains from Alcippa's peculiar mode of kissing evoke no compensating effects in Lacon's couplet, which crudely attempts to improve on it by asserting success in love, in language which, first substituting the rhetorical 'bestowed' for Comatas' 'gave', ends in a bathetically wordy half line. In a parting thrust, Comatas gleefully claims the victory, which Morson immediately awards to him. Calling on his herd to celebrate with him, and with appropriate strictures on the behaviour of the billy-goat—the reference to Melanthius is a vague oath, implying 'or I'll be castrated myself', for at *Odyssey* 22.475 the traitor-goatherd Melanthius is killed by Odysseus in a peculiarly bloody manner—Comatas departs to sacrifice to the nymphs, the poet leaving us with a strong impression, not merely of the bonds of sympathy between man and beast, as in Idylls IV and VI, but of man's instinctual affinity with the beasts when all his gentler attributes of love, friendship, reverence, and courtesy are denied.

The Shepherd and the Goatherd

(Comatas, Lacon, Morson)

COMATAS

My nannies, keep your distance from that shepherd there,
    Lacon—
A Sybarite, as he likes to think! He stole my goatskin
    yesterday.

LACON

Psst! my lambs, get away from the spring there! Don't you
    see
the man who stole my pipes the other day—Comatas?

COMATAS

Pipes! What pipes? Since when did you, Sibyrtas' slave,
own such a thing as pipes? Is it not good enough for you
    nowadays,
that straw whistle you used to toot on, in Corydon's
    company?

LACON

That Lycon gave me, so please your honour! But what
    sort of goatskin
can I have lifted from you? Answer me that, Comatas!
Why, not even Eumaras, your master, has one to sleep in.   10

COMATAS

The brindled skin that Crocylus gave me when he offered
    the goat
to the nymphs—and you, you dog, were eating your heart
    out then
with envy, and now you're making an end—stripping me
    skinless!

LACON

I never—by Pan of the Headland himself I swear Lacon,
son of Calaethis, never did take your cloak. If I lie, my dear
    friend,
may I go off my head and jump in the Crathis, over those
    cliffs there!

COMATAS

And neither did I—I swear by the nymphs of this spring,
    dear sir,
as I hope their favour and kindness may follow me
    evermore—
Comatas never did pinch any pipes of yours on the sly.

LACON

20 If I believe you, the pains of Daphnis smite me!
But if you care to stake a kid—it's no great stakes—
I'm happy to bandy verses with you until you've your
    bellyful!

COMATAS

A pig, they say, once challenged Athene! There's my kid.
How about a lamb for *your* wager—and not too skinny?

LACON

Smart, aren't you! Are those fair terms? Is there anyone
shears hairs for fleeces, or when a goat stands by
with her first kid, prefers to milk a bloody bitch?

COMATAS

Yes—one full of conceit, as you when you challenge me!
A wasp buzzing against a cicada! But since the kid
doesn't live up to your standards—the goat himself!
30   Begin!

LACON

No hurry—not on fire, are you? You'll sing the sweeter
if you'll sit over here, under the wild olive and those
taller trees, where the stream flows cool. There's growing
grass, and this hay here, and here the crickets are chirruping.

COMATAS

I'm in no hurry; I'm merely pained that you should dare
look me straight in the face—I who was once your teacher,
when you were still a child! See what gratitude you get!
As well raise wolves—'Raise dogs', they say, 'to eat you!'

LACON

And when do I recall your teaching or even telling me
a thing of the slightest value—a mean little sod like you?   40

COMATAS

That's one lesson you'll remember my giving you—you
    got a pain,
and even these nannies bleated—the goat dug into them!

LACON

May they dig no deeper when they bury you, you hump-
    backed bugger!
Crawl over here, then—crawl, to sing your final match!

COMATAS

That I won't. On my side are oaks and galingale,
and the bees are making a wonderful humming about the
    hives.
There are two springs of cold water here, and the birds
twitter in the treetops, and the shade's beyond compare
better than on your side, and the pine tree showers us with
    cones.

LACON
If you'll come over by me, it's lambskins you shall have,
I promise,
under your feet, and fleeces softer than sleep. They stink,
those goats beside you, even worse than you do yourself.
And I'll provide a great bowl of white milk,
an offering to the nymphs, and another of the mildest olive
oil.

COMATAS
And if you'll move over here, you'll tread on soft fern
and pennyroyal in flower, and under your feet I'll lay
goatskins, four times softer than those skins of lambs
you brag of. Eight pails of milk I'll set out, too,
for Pan, and eight dishes of comb, running with honey.

LACON
Fine—you can sing a round with me right where you are!
You can keep
your oaks, and tread on your own ground! But who shall
decide
between us? I wish the cowherd Lycopas would come this
way.

COMATAS
I could do without him. But if you wish, we could shout
to that man,
that woodcutter chopping the heather near you—why, it's
Morson!

LACON
Let's give him a shout.

COMATAS
Go on, then, call him.

LACON
> Hey!
friend, come over here and listen to us for a bit:
we're holding a trial, which can compose the best couplets,
country-style. And remember, good Morson, you mustn't
  be partial
to me, and make very sure you're not over-generous to
  him!

COMATAS
That's right, by the nymphs, dear Morson: you mustn't
  give more than my due   70
to me, and make very sure you don't give preference to
  him!
You should know, by the way, that these flocks belong to
  Sibyrtas of Thurii
and the goats you see here, friend, are owned by the
  Sybarite Eumaras.

LACON
Did anyone ask you, you evil old man, whether these flocks
belong to Sibyrtas or me? God, what a gossip you are!

COMATAS
My excellent friend, I'm not attempting to score off you—
merely telling the truth. You're over-fond of a brawl.

LACON
All right—start, if you've anything to start with. Our
  friend will want
to get back to the city alive. Apollo, but you're a windbag!

(*they sing*)

COMATAS
The Muses love me much more than the minstrel Daphnis,   80
for I sacrificed two kids to them the other day.

LACON

Ah, but Apollo loves me dearly: I am rearing
a fine ram for him: the Carnea's coming along.

COMATAS

All but two of my goats have twins, and as I milk them,
'Poor thing, you need a helper,' the maid says, with a look.

LACON

Chicken feed! Lacon has cheese enough to fill almost
    twenty
baskets—and he debauches a beardless boy in the
    shrubbery.

COMATAS

As the goatherd drives his goats past her, Clearista
pelts him with apples and come-hither noises—ever so
    sweet!

LACON

When Cratidas runs, so smooth, to meet the shepherd—
90   me—
he maddens me, the way he shakes the bright mane on his
    neck!

COMATAS

Ah, but your dogrose and windflower are not to be
    compared
with the rose that is grown in beds, under sheltering walls.

LACON

Nor are my medlars to be compared with your acorns.
    They
have a thin rind of the wood of the oak, but mine are
    honied.

COMATAS
I will go and catch a ringdove, to give my girl as a present:
I will take it out of the juniper bush, where it is perching.

LACON
And I, when I shear the black ewe, will give its fleece,
my own gift, to Cratidas, to make him a warm cloak.

COMATAS
Psst!—get away from the olive grove, my kids, and come   100
over here to graze, at the foot of the hill, where the myrtles
   are.

LACON
Won't you get out of that oak copse, Conarus and Cinaetha,
and come over here to browse, on the east side, with
   Phalarus?

COMATAS
I have a pitcher of cypress wood, and also a bowl,
a genuine Praxiteles. I'm keeping both for my girl.

LACON
And I have a shepherd dog, a breed that can throttle a wolf:
that's what I'm giving my boy, to hunt every beast he
   pleases.

COMATAS
You locusts, who go hopping over my vineyard wall,
spare to ravish my vines, all in the bloom of their youth!

LACON
You cicadas, you see how I'm setting the pace for this
   goatherd here: 110
so does your ceaseless singing set the pace for the gleaners.

COMATAS

How I hate the shagtailed foxes, who come creeping up
and into Nicon's place at evening, pilfering the grapes!

LACON

And my especial bugbear is a kind of flying beetle:
the wind blows them in, and they blight Philondas' figs.

COMATAS

I suppose you've forgotten the ploughing I gave you, and
how you smirked
and wiggled away with your hips, hanging onto that oak
tree?

LACON

Afraid I have. But I'll tell you what I well remember:
how Eumaras tied you to that tree and gave you a dusting
down.

COMATAS

Morson, here's someone getting a little galled! You
observed?
Would you kindly run to a witch's grave and pick us some
squills.

120

LACON

I too seem to be acting the irritant, you'll have noticed,
Morson! Go to the Haleis and pull up a cyclamen root.

COMATAS

Himera might well with milk instead of water. Crathis,
you might run red wine, your reeds bear fruits. . . .

LACON

Sybaris might gush honey for us, and at dawn
the girl might fill her pail with honeycomb, for water. . . .

COMATAS
Moon-trefoil and goatweed are food for goats of mine:
they trample upon mastic and lie upon arbutus.

LACON
Well, but my ewes have balm on which to browse,   130
and the dogrose blossoms in plenty, like the rose itself.

COMATAS
I do not love Alcippa, for yesterday she did not take me
by the ears and kiss me, when I gave her the ringdove.

LACON
But I do love Eumedes, dearly: when my bounty
bestowed a pipe upon him, his kiss was really something!

COMATAS
Lacon, heaven forbids jays to vie with nightingales,
or hoopoes swans: but you, you fool, must have a brawl.

MORSON
My verdict is, the shepherd must throw in. To you,
Comatas, Morson awards the lamb. When you've sacrificed
to the nymphs, you will see that you send a choice cut to
    Morson.   140

COMATAS
By Pan, I will. Now you can caper, billies all!
I'm going to laugh my bellyful at shepherd Lacon—watch
    me!—
just as soon as I've dispatched his lamb. You'll see me leap
to heaven! Cheers, my horny beauties! Tomorrow I'll
    bathe
each girl of you in Sybaris' lake. Hey, you, the white one—
Butter Boy! If you ride a single nanny before

I sacrifice to the nymphs, you'll feel my knife. He's at it
   again!
If I don't castrate you, I'll be called Melanthius, not
   Comatas!

᪥Idyll VI

This poem, using the familiar device of the song within the idyll, presents two motifs: that of the herdsmen Daphnis and Damoetas, which forms the main account or 'frame', and that of Polyphemus and Galatea, of whom they sing, and which may be referred to as the 'inset'. Moreover, the address to Theocritus' friend Aratus introduces a third dimension, a context for the whole composition; but while its theme may have some particular relevance to Aratus' affairs, as Idyll XII has to Nicias', this cannot now be known, and it is in any case quite as likely that Aratus is named with no significance beyond that of a general dedication. Certainly there is no warrant here for extracting a 'message' as we do from the contents of Simichidas' song in Idyll VII.

It will further become apparent that this Idyll can hardly be appreciated out of the context of other of the bucolic Idylls, and forms a clear example of the sort of interrelationship of theme which could indicate that a number of these were issued as a unified work. Neither the manuscript evidence nor internal indications give grounds for precision, but we may suppose with some probability that Idylls I, III, IV, V, VI, and VII (not necessarily in that order), with the more tentative additions of II, X, and XI, fall into the same group.

The frame of the present Idyll relates how the youthful Daphnis (the same, we cannot doubt, as the legendary hero whose death is related in Thyrsis' song) and the still younger Damoetas, also a cowherd, happened to drive their flocks to the same spot. To anyone familiar with Greek literature, the mention of their respective stages of growth at once suggests some form of love relationship, and this is borne out by the kiss that concludes their singing. Daphnis has challenged Damoetas, and they sit down together in an agreeable place to hold a singing contest. This may be no more than a pleasant method of whiling away the noonday heat, but there is perhaps a hint that Daphnis, as challenger, is prompted by more than musical emulation, that there is some underlying significance to the exercise that the participants understand and the audience is invited to share.

We recall that in Idyll V the singing contest was a means of settling scores. In that Idyll, too, a love relationship, though of an animal sort, was discovered to have existed between the contestants, who encounter each other with accusation and taunts and quarrel over the stakes and the location of their contest. This takes a cut-and-thrust form, with the aim of galling each other, and when Comatas, who takes on the role of the injured party and challenger (see the introduction to Idyll V), is pronounced victor, he calls on his herd to exult with him over the defeated Lacon. The present Idyll forms a distinct contrast: there is accord over the place for singing; the two sit down together; there are no stakes, but at the end a spontaneous exchange of pipes. Further emphasizing their unity of spirit, the youths play together on the pipes, and their herds, sharing of their own accord the lovers' joy, dance to the music they make. The lesson becomes explicit in the closing line. Assuming a measure of initial disharmony between the herdsmen (not the hostility of Comatas and Lacon, but rather an uncertainty as to how far they are in accord), we may conclude that the elder has wished to make trial of the younger's worthiness, and Damoetas, by his graceful responsiveness, has proved himself Daphnis' peer.

As is only appropriate to a love trial, the inset deals also with the theme of love, but with a dissatisfying and discordant affair, that between the Cyclops Polyphemus (best known from his more horrific appearance in the *Odyssey*) and the sea nymph Galatea. The fact that a heterosexual affair is here in question is probably not important. Although Theocritus' personal love songs are to boys, he does not, to judge from his works, consider homosexual love as necessarily the more exalted passion: his theme, repeatedly, is the evil effects of Eros wherever he enters into human relationships. In the present Idyll it is two males who seem likely to achieve the most harmonious love relationship to be found in Theocritus, and which we may therefore term 'idyllic', in contrast to the wilfully 'crossed' love of Polyphemus and Galatea; but Theocritus' use of the legend of Daphnis' death in Idylls I and VII shows that an exalted, desperate, spiritual love can, for him, be heterosexual. Idyll V makes it clear that the homosexual relationship can, in Theocritus' view, be brutal and animalistic, while the heterosexual appears as animalistic, though not brutal, in the reference to the old man and the girl in Idyll IV. Idyll VII depicts two homosexual loves: Lycidas', which is spiritual and aspires beyond easy attainment, and Aratus', which is prosaic and a cause hardly worth wearing oneself out over. In the same Idyll it is Simichidas' love for a courtesan which is satisfying, because practical and unsentimental. All in all, we cannot say that Theocritus gives clear theoretical ranking to either Eros-of-women or Eros-of-boys.

The characters of Galatea and Polyphemus, as displayed in turn by Daphnis and Damoetas in their matched poems, reveal the psychological causes for which their relationship must ever remain futile and unconcluded. Galatea is 'light as thistledown', petulant and unstable, while Polyphemus is self-satisfied and fatuously complacent about his physical attractiveness (though this one-eyed shepherd's suit of the 'brittle' nymph recalls Idyll III—with the difference that there the goatherd is miserably self-conscious about his shortcomings). Between these empty characters there is no accommodation. This is symbolized by the fact (emphasized in Idyll XI, but also included here in the words 'on this isle') that the sea is her native element, the land his, and neither can—or will, which in terms of Theocritus' fatalistic psychology is much the same thing—leave his own for the other's. But the exercise of developing these attitudes in song acts precisely as an accommodation for those who participate in it. So Daphnis, in narrating Galatea's conduct towards Polyphemus, displays a solicitude for her which we may take to be a hint to his own beloved not to hurt them both by 'lightness'. And Damoetas closes his own parable, with its implicit warning to Daphnis not to pretend aloofness, with the kiss of conciliation. The 'moral' of their tale communicates itself between the singers, and expresses their will to avoid all such vanity.

Damoetas and Daphnis

It happened one day, Aratus, that Daphnis the herdsman
drove his kine to the selfsame spot as Damoetas.
On Daphnis' cheek was the golden flower of manhood;
Damoetas' beard was already halfway grown.
They sat down by a well to sing—it was summer and
　　midday—
and Daphnis began the match, for he first had desired it.

DAPHNIS
Galatea is pelting your flocks, Polyphemus, with apples,
and calling you names—goatherd and laggard in love;
and you, poor fool, do not see, but sit sweetly piping.
Look, there again! She's hurling one at your sheepdog,　　10
and the bitch is looking out to sea and barking—
you can see her silhouetted on the clear of the waves,
as she runs along the edge of the gently sucking sands.
Watch out that she doesn't rush at the child's knees,
emerging from the water, and claw her fairy flesh!
She's casting at you again, look— brittle as the down
the torrid glare of summer leaves upon the thistle.
You love, she flees; and when you leave loving, follows,
staking her all upon a desperate move. Ah, Love!
How often, Polyphemus, has he made unfair show fair!　　20

Then Damoetas lifted up his voice and sang.

DAMOETAS
I saw, yes, by Pan, I saw when she pelted the flock.
It did not escape me—no, by my one sweet eye:
may I see with it to the last, and may Prophet Telamus
　　carry
his hostile mouthings home, to keep for his children!
But I too can use the goad, so I take no notice,
and tell her I've another woman now. Apollo!

Hearing that, she's all consumed with spite,
and frenziedly spies, from the sea, on my cave and flocks.
30   It was I set on the dog to bark at her, too.
In the days of my courting, it used to lay its muzzle
against her groin and whine. When she's seen enough
of this act of mine, perhaps she'll send a messenger;
but I'll bar my door, until she vows in person
to make my bed up fairly on this isle.
Certainly I'm not ugly, as they call me;
for lately I looked in the sea—there was a calm—
and I thought my cheeks and my one eye showed up
    handsome,
and my teeth shone back, whiter than Parian marble.
40   But I spat three times into my bosom,
as the witch Cotyttaris taught me, to turn away evil.

When he had done, Damoetas kissed Daphnis
and gave him a pipe, and a fine flute Daphnis gave.
Damoetas fluted and herdsman Daphnis piped,
and the heifers began to prance on the soft sward.
Neither was victor; both unvanquished proved.

❧Idyll VII

This Idyll is singular. At first sight it narrates an incident in Theocritus' life, a journey 'I' made with two companions from the city of Cos to a farm in the country, to be guests at a harvest-home celebration. But the bulk of the poem is concerned with a strange, though apparently not unexpected, encounter with a goatherd, who, after greeting the author not as 'Theocritus' but as 'Simichidas', pronounces on contemporary literary controversy and, being invited, sings an impassioned and exquisite song, to which the traveller matches one from his own repertory. If suspicions are aroused by this peculiar and apparently disjointed treatment of so simple and even trivial a theme, it is with reason, for the poem, as will appear, is by no means to be classed with those 'occasional' pieces which refer to episodes in Theocritus' experience (Idylls XII and XXVIII–XXXI), but is autobiographical in a more essential way. It is in fact a revelation of the author precisely *qua* poet, made through the medium of the bucolic art which was his own, and of which it stands as perhaps the most highly wrought and significant exemplar.

We may begin with the goatherd Lycidas, who, deliberately depicted as enigmatic, seems to have been designed to pose a riddle even to contemporaries. Modern speculation has centred round Theocritus' oddly emphatic assertion that 'he was a goatherd, nor could anyone who saw him have mistaken the fact, since he was exactly like a goatherd'—words which have been taken as meaning either that Lycidas is or that he is not in fact a goatherd; either he is a poet whose whim it is to dress like a goatherd, or—taking Theocritus' statement at its most literal—he is a goatherd who happens also to be a consummate poet.*

*See Archibald Cameron, 'The Form of the Thalysia', in *Miscellanea di Studi Alessandrini in memoria di Augusto Rostagni*, pp. 291–307 (Turin: B. d'Erasmo,

One explanation, long favoured, was that there was a coterie of poets on Cos who adopted rustic garb and engaged in country-style singing contests under assumed names. Thus Simichidas (the etymology suggests 'snub-nosed', which reminds one of the goatherd of Idyll III) would be Theocritus' rustic alias, and Lycidas that of another poet here masquerading as a goatherd. The theory has been abandoned, to be replaced by a modification: Lycidas is an alias for a known poet—not, however, known to the ancient commentators, who have left us notes on the names Simichidas and Sicelidas, but not on Lycidas—and his depiction as a goatherd is a whim or jest of Theocritus', perhaps in reference to something in his works.

Perhaps the most plausible of the identifications which have been made for Lycidas is with the poet Leonidas of Tarentum.* The arguments are far from conclusive, but the conjectures on

---

1963); Cameron gives a summary of the chief representatives of the various interpretations of Lycidas.

*R. J. Cholmeley, *The Idylls of Theocritus*, 2nd ed. (London: G. Bell and Sons, (1919), pp. 18–20. Cholmeley sets out the arguments for this identification (which he considers 'certain') in his introduction. It was first made by P.E. Legrand, *Étude sur Théocrite* (Paris: A. Fontemoing, 1898). Briefly, it runs as follows: Leonidas—a very common Greek name in its more familiar Attic form, Leonides—means 'Son of the Lion', and so might be represented by the pseudonym Lycidas, which means 'Son of the Wolf'. Remarkably, Callimachus, in his twenty-second Epigram, refers to a certain 'Astacides, the Cretan, the goatherd'. Now 'Astacides', from a rare word, has the same meaning as 'Leonidas'. Though a Tarentine by birth, Leonidas appears to have spent some time on the island of Crete, and the Cydonia mentioned by Theocritus in connection with Lycidas is very probably Cydonia in Crete—though other ancient towns of the name are known. In other words, Lycidas, the goatherd of Cydonia, may refer to the same man as 'Astacides, the Cretan, the goatherd', of Callimachus' poem. However, if the latter predates Idyll VII, we might have expected Theocritus to use the established pseudonym 'Astacides' for Leonidas, as he uses 'Sicelides' for Asclepiades. A certain quantity of Leonidas' poems survive, and they not infrequently have a country setting (not that they are 'pastoral' in the sense that Theocritus brought to the tradition; see General Introduction, p. 12). We further know that Leonidas was a poor wanderer who might well have turned up on Cos and been dressed like a rustic, but we have no grounds (other than the identifications with Astacides and Lycidas of Callimachus' and Theocritus' poems) for supposing that he was a goatherd or would have been dressed like one.

which they rest have a certain attractiveness, and form a better basis for actual identification of Lycidas than others that have been proposed. Yet if Theocritus was thinking of Leonidas, he concealed him more effectively than the other poets mentioned in Idyll VII, including himself, who is clearly in some way to be identified with Simichidas. The song put into the mouth of Lycidas cannot be supposed to be by anyone but Theocritus himself; nor, it should be emphasized, does it resemble anything that we know of the work of Leonidas, which seems to have been characterized by a realistic, not an idealizing tone. It remains possible—and indeed may seem a likely explanation, taking all the evidence into account—that Theocritus intended a graceful bow in the direction of Leonidas, as to one to whom he was initially indebted for his pastoral *maîtrise*—but a bow discreet enough not to distract from the prime significance of Lycidas in the poem. In other words, the simple equation Lycidas = Leonidas would be as naive as Simichidas = Theocritus.

Another line of interpretation holds that both Lycidas and Simichidas are symbolic characters who hold conversation in Theocritus' imagination as he journeys.* All in all and bearing in mind the Hellenistic Age's capacity for a symbolism scarcely less sophisticated than that of our own, only a private, mental interpretation will do justice to Theocritus' account of the meeting of these two characters. We shall do well to follow in this direction.

At the outset one is struck by the lack of contact between Lycidas and Theocritus' companions. True, there is the initial plural verb 'we met', but thereafter they are no more mentioned, and are likely to drop from the reader's field of vision, as they apparently have from that of Theocritus-Simichidas, until after the departure of Lycidas, who likewise has no part in the ostensible object of their journey. The plural verb is no great obstacle:

---

*J. H. Kühn, 'Die Thalysien Theokrits', *Hermes* 86(1958):40–79. Kühn regards Lycidas as personifying Theocritus' bucolic ideal, as distinct from his realistic poetic character (personified in Simichidas). This, however, leaves out of account the significance of the olive staff, which is crucial to my interpretation.

it may be viewed as a literary *façon de parler*, and indeed this 'writer's "we"' appears eighteen lines later in the Greek. Moreover it softens the transition from the journey of the three to the encounter one-to-one. The singular here would have alerted the reader that something strange was afoot, perhaps giving the game away too easily and leaving too little to tease sophisticated wits; and in any case it would have run counter to the tradition stemming from mythology and Homer whereby visitants from another realm are encountered 'naturally'. This convention needs to be borne in mind, for it is in keeping with it that this encounter is set in a specified locality, on a route which may still be traced and which is indicated in the poem by such concrete landmarks as Brasilas' tomb and Mount Oromedon. (Contrasting with this solidity of detail is the miraculous account, soon after the poem opens, of the origin of Bourina Spring, the effect of which is to prepare for the supernatural mood dominating the poem.)

Certain other details also are in keeping with the conventions surrounding supernatural visitations: the point of encounter, 'about half way'; the magic hour of noon (cf. Idyll I); the characteristically Homeric language; the suddenness, and yet the natural manner of Lycidas' arrival and departure; his leaving a significant token with Simichidas.* We may compare the encounter of Odysseus with Hermes in Book X of the *Odyssey*: the mode is 'natural', and the god, after instructing Odysseus, departs, leaving behind the gift of moly. Or the meeting of the poet Hesiod with the Muses, which he describes at the outset of his *Works and Days* as taking place on a hillside—a later tradition readily supplied midday as the hour—and their gift to him of poetic inspiration. Both these earlier examples may be readily demythologized, the gods being viewed as forces at work in the psyche and the gift of moly as a palpable sign that forewarned is forearmed. The step to a conscious mythologizing of abstract forces is the step from the heroic to the Hellenistic Age (see the introductions to Idylls I and II.)

---

*See Cameron, 'The Form of the Thalysia', pp. 293–300, for a full treatment of the convention.

Lycidas' gift of his staff of wild olive is, in keeping with the age, explicitly symbolic. He says it is 'from the Muses'—which phrase, as is intended, immediately recalls Hesiod. The olive, Athene's tree, denotes wisdom. This, significantly, is the wild variety—all in all, an appropriately bucolic gift. Rustic-wisdom-'from the Muses' adds up to bucolic inspiration. Simichidas, in introducing his song, has already claimed an earlier initiation 'from the nymphs', but the gift from Lycidas marks a consummation. Henceforth he is endowed with the 'strain of higher mood' which is in the gift of the Muses and their emissary, Lycidas. That Lycidas is no less is clear on several counts. He is introduced as 'noble with the Muses', which might be paraphrased 'of a virtue derived from the Muses'. He ends his song —the very exemplar of the 'higher mood' pastoral—with his admiration, almost worship, for the 'divine Comatas', another poet-goatherd, who was nourished on honey (a clear symbol) sent by the Muses, and whom we may suppose to have been Lycidas' own master in song.* Finally, by a nice irony, Lycidas belongs to the Muses as himself a projection of Theocritus' poetic inspiration—a *double entendre* which we ought not to suppose would have been lost on a Hellenistic audience, and which the phrase 'noble with the Muses' may include.

The stick motif will provide another clue. The olive stick is not, as has been supposed, a reward for winning a singing match; it is not even clear that a match is in question here—if it is, the element of rivalry is minimal. Nor is it promised conditionally on Simichidas' equalling Lycidas' art (for it is not clear that he does, the poems being designedly disparate, and Simichidas' lower in theme) but, as Lycidas' words make clear, on his displaying poetic integrity, in contrast to the vain toilings of the imitators of Homer. The height of bucolic inspiration is to be Simichidas' reward for the good use he has made of the Muses' gift hitherto—a prowess he himself claims to be only moder-

---

*Indeed, we seem to be presented with a regress in symbolic fantasy, the legendary Comatas standing behind the semi-real Lycidas as he stands behind the realistic Simichidas—and, we might even add, he behind the real Theocritus!

ate. This is the hope of equalling Lycidas to which he refers, and while his subsequent remark that his reputation 'may have reached to the throne of Zeus' may be, as is generally held, a hint to the reigning Ptolemy, to whom he appeals for patronage in Idyll XVII, at its face value it is an intimation that Simichidas understands the reason for the visitation of Lycidas, for the Muses are daughters of Zeus (cf. Idyll XVI).

Lycidas, then, is placed squarely in a country context. He 'is' a goatherd, and, as has been well observed, his smile and twinkling eyes (to which attention is drawn repeatedly) and his mocking manner ally him with the figure of the satyr in contemporary art (not the lewd goblins of an earlier age, but their politer descendants, the little goat-men, familiars of the Hellenistic landscape, who make 'artless' music, learned from nature, upon their reed pipes).* The comparison is not to be pressed: Lycidas is more than a satyr, as his poetic criticism and the studied accomplishment of his own composition make clear. It is made solely to show how these physical traits, as his garb and also his name, indicate his connection with wild nature. His song is natural in the simplicity of its passions: his erotic longing for Ageanax, his worship of Comatas; but nature is transcended, and elevated by the human spirit into what we have already recognized as bucolic art. So Lycidas envisages celebrating the attainment of his love, in signification of fidelity and joy in the beloved. So he yearns to pasture the ideal herd of Comatas in an ideal landscape and listen to the ideal song of this archetypal goatherd-poet. The illustrative details, too, are romanticized, though drawn from nature. The sea voyage to Mitylene, on Lesbos, island of Sappho, of poetry and of love, takes on an erotic significance which is commonplace in ancient literature, and the halcyons that can calm its storms are Aphrodite's own birds. Romantic too is the evocation of the sea, with its winds and its wastes and its dwellers, mortal and immortal. And the goatherd's beloved bears an aristocratic-sounding name. The real and the ideal country life are indeed drawn together in the

*See Lawall, *Theocritus' Coan Pastorals*, p. 85.

songs about ideal herdsmen that real herdsmen, with names derived from down-to-earth localities and occupations (for Tityrus see Idyll III), will sing at Lycidas' solitary love feast. And Daphnis, whom nature mourned, is surely intended to recall Idyll I, Theocritus' own most perfect essay in the bucolic art he took to himself, on what may well be the historical occasion of this walk through the countryside. Hitherto Theocritus has been plain Simichidas, the 'snub-nosed', who enters the poem coming from the city, and wearing citified boots, to Lycidas' amusement. His song, too, treats of the typical city love affair, with its *paraclausithuron* (see introduction to Idyll III), in aid of a real person, the poet's friend Aratus. Its object is seen in very pragmatic terms as the satisfaction of sexual desire. Aratus' passion is located in his bowels and bones. In fact none-too-pleasant physical allusions throughout serve to keep the tone very unsublimated indeed, from the sneezing of the Erotes in the first line to the witch's spitting in the last. So Simichidas' happy (because realistic) passion for a courtesan is goatlike; the tortures to be inflicted on Pan (goatherd-deity and satyr in chief) if he heed not Aratus' prayer, or to be spared him if he grant it, are made none the less graphic for the display of antiquarian and geographic lore. Aratus may comfort himself that Philinus' beauty is already past its prime and that once his bloom has faded, he can be forgotten. And courtship is a wearisome and footsore business. The contrast in tone with Lycidas' poem could hardly be more complete.

But the goal of Simichidas' journey is the farm of some friends, gentlemen of breeding, as we have learned. It is neither town nor country, though set in the country and at a good remove from the town. And it is a place, precisely, for the cultivation by art of wild nature: so the fruits of the festival contrast with the wild flowers of Lycidas' imagined rustic love feast, the prime setting for idyllic tales. In the poet's highly subjective and symbolic account of the festival, the wine that the nymphs of the Castalian Spring (on Parnassus, Apollo's mountain) 'set welling' for him is already, as a natural juice needing man's cultivation, a fit symbol of poetic inspiration. In particular it symbolizes the plain style of Simichidas-Theocritus, now 'cultivated' by the newly acquired bequest from Lycidas of the highly wrought, idealizing lyric style to bring about the transformation he is here celebrating. Moreover, the verb I have rendered as 'set welling' is found only here in Greek literature, and is composed of a preposition meaning 'apart'—suggesting two objects—and a poetic word connected with the Greek for 'a spring'. Taken with the identification of the nymphs, this appears to be a strong hint that water, and specifically that from the spring associated with Apollo—hence poetic inspiration—is involved as well as wine; and we recall that the ancients were accustomed to mix them. Here too is an image of the commingling of styles, of the plain, pure country water springing from Parnassus with the headier wine of man's contriving. We should note that neither the wine nor the water can be precisely squared with the plain and the lyric styles we are taking them to represent; they overlap, each symbol containing elements of both—as indeed must the poetic productions they represent in some degree exhibit them both: and this analysis, be it further noted, offers us a good example of the poetic symbol in its integrity, rich in suggestion and unable to be too precisely pinned down.

The same living, fertile quality is to be perceived in the mythological comparisons Theocritus adduces to fill out the significance of the wine of the festival. These cannot but evoke violence and bloodshed, for the wine offered by Chiron to Heracles led the latter to let fly an arrow which killed his host, while the wine Odysseus gave Polyphemus enabled him to blind the Cyclops.* Latent seems to be a suggestion that the human cultivation which is crowned by poetry is purchased at a price.

It is doubtful if this sombre echo, which sounds strangely amid the festive ending of a poem so full of joy and optimism, rises from any conscious level of the poet's mind; at all events Theocritus in both cases leaves the tragedy unuttered, using the myths overtly as illustration of the potency of wine, which overcomes even the strong like Heracles and Polyphemus. Moreover

*This was drawn to my attention by an anonymous reader of the manuscript for the University of North Carolina Press, to whom I am grateful for thus leading me to give further consideration to the whole passage.

it seems that he has in mind Euripides' 'satyric' version of Polyphemus, with its emphasis on the more human qualities of the Cyclops, rather than Homer's. In this connection we may recall Theocritus' own gentler versions of Polyphemus in Idylls VI and XI and his clear dependence on Euripides in Idyll XXVI.

A more prominent poetic motive for the introduction of the centaurs and the Cyclops is that they are the uncouth representatives of wild nature while the heroes represent man: thus the myths illustrate—as is the function of myths—the relations between man and the world in which he finds himself. In the one, nature has the guise of the benign host inadvertently destroyed by the guest he has entertained; in the other, the menacing host is destroyed by the man in self-defence. The parallelism is not complete and we should not strain it in an attempt to find it so. Theocritus asks us only to note that in both, wine, the cheering and intoxicating drink to which both nature and man contribute their part, plays a key role in controlling the destinies of men. Here the actual wine of the festival is thought of as in some way prepared—perhaps tempered with Castalian water—by Apollo's nymphs, and so becomes a symbol of poetic inspiration; and at this point we recall that the myths are themselves the products of cultivation by poets. Thus the symbol perfectly unites the concrete world with that of the spirit, so that we perceive the real and the symbolic wine as the divine power whereby Theocritus is enabled to praise Demeter, goddess of the products of man's cultivation, for his own poetic harvest predicted by Lycidas. We leave him triumphant and—with a touch of yearning which echoes the ending of Lycidas' song—hoping for beatitude renewed.

The Harvest Home

It happened one time that we left the city and hied
to the Haleis, Eucritus and I and Amyntas our third.
A harvest home was being held for Demeter
by Phrasidamus and Antigenes, sons of Lycopeus—
a noble line if ever there was one, sprung
from ancient worthies, Clyteia and Chalcon himself,
who grappled well the rock with his knee, and well
drew out Bourina Spring with a blow of his foot—
whereon elm and poplar, beginning rear
10 luxuriant crests aloft of green-leaf hair,
all over-wove, of shadow-threads, a grove. . . .
Our journey was not half done, nor had we yet
Brasilas' tomb in sight, when we met with a wayfarer,
thanks to the Muses, a noble fellow, by name
Lycidas, of Cydonia, and you could tell at a glance
he was a goatherd; he fitted the part completely:
on his shoulders, a hairy, mustard-coloured goatskin,
smelling of new-set curds; an elderly smock
fastened over his breast with a broad band;
20 in his hand a crooked stick of wild olive wood.
In a gently mocking voice, with eyes sparkling
and laughter clinging round his lips, he said to me,
'Simichidas, where do your feet draw you this noontide,
when the very lizard's asleep in the crack of the wall,
and the deathshead swifts not at their wheeling?
Are you speeding to dine where you've not been asked, or
    running
to some burgher's winepress gates? Why, at every step
the pebbles sing out one by one as they bounce off your
    boots!'
I answered him, 'Friend Lycidas, all tell me you are
30 a piper without all peer among herdsmen or reapers.
And happy I am to hear it—yet I've a lurking
hope I may prove your equal. We go this road
to a harvest home: some gentlemen, friends of ours,

are honouring fair-robed Demeter with the first fruits
of her largesse, who has heaped their threshing floor
with a rollicking measure of barley! I pray you then,
the way is ours and ours the day: let's sing
country-style: the pleasure may well be mutual.
I too am a sounding reed of the Muses, and called by all
an excellent poet—though Zeus knows, I'm no gull!   40
I am not, in my own conceit, a match as yet
for the noble Samian Sicelidas, nor Philetas.
I should rival their song as a frog vies with cicadas!'
So I spoke, with design, and merrily laughed the goatherd.
'I shall present you with my olive stick', said he,
'For a young sprig fashioned by Zeus, with no pretensions!
How I hate the builder who seeks to raise his house
as high as the peak of Mount Oromedon there,
and the Muses' cuckoos, with their eye on the bard of
    Chios!
In vain they labour. . . ! But let us begin the singing,   50
Simichidas: I propose. . . . See here, friend, if you like
a trifling thing I laboured over lately on the hillside.

'Fair sail shall Ageanax have to Mitylene
when the wet sou'wester chases the waves to where
the Kids set in the evening, and Orion
in the morning plants his feet on the ocean floor. . . .
Fair sail shall Ageanax have to Mitylene—
so he but save Lycidas from Aphrodite's oven,
for the love of him is the hot blast that consumes me!
Ah, the halcyons shall stroke to sleep the sea waves,   60
Notus allaying and Eurus, who stirs the weeds
in the depths—the halcyons, birds of the wraith nymphs
most loved, and of those whose catch is from the sea. . . .
May Ageanax, seeking crossing to Mitylene,
find all weather to his turn and reach his haven
after a safe voyage. I on that day
shall sport a wreath of anise flowers, or roses,
or snowdrops, round my brow, and by the fire

reclining, drink off a cask of Ptelean wine,
70   with a servant by to roast me beans on the hearth.
My couch shall be heaped cubit-deep with fleabane,
and asphodel, and crinkled celery, and sweet
the draughts I'll quaff, pledging to mind his name,
Ageanax, in every cup, and thrusting out
my lip to the lees. Two shepherds shall pipe to me,
one of Acharnae, one of Lycopas, and Tityrus
nearby will sing of how, when Daphnis the herd
loved Xenea once, the hills around
groaned, and the oaks that grow on Himera's banks
80   mourned him, the while he wasted like the snows
below rearing Haemus, Athos, Rhodope
or remotest Caucasus lying. And he shall sing
of the goatherd enclosed in a great coffer, alive,
by his wicked master's presumption: the snub-nosed bees
fed him from bland flowers, hieing from the meadow
to the fragrant cedar chest, for the Muse had honied
nectar spilt on his lips. O bless'd Comatas!
Yours was this happy ordeal, to be penned in the chest
and labour one yearlong spring, on honeycomb fed!
90   Would, in my day, you were numbered among the living;
then would I herd your fine goats on the hillsides
and listen to your voice, as you lay and warbled sweetly
under the oaks or pines, divine Comatas!'

So much he spoke and ceased. I in my turn
addressed him thus: 'Lycidas, friend, I too
have herding on the mountains learned from the nymphs
many a noble theme—it may be fame
has borne them even to the throne of Zeus! But this
I shall regale you with is by far the foremost.
100   Hear me, then, for dear you prove to the Muses.
'The Loves have sneezed for Simichidas. Poor wretch,
Myrto I love, as the goats love the spring.
But Aratus, dearest of men to me, harbours the sting
of desire in his bowels for a boy—witness the noblest

of gentlemen, Aristis, whom Apollo himself
would not begrudge to stand with his lyre and sing
beside his Delphian tripods—witness, Aristis,
how Aratus burns to the marrow with love for a boy!
Pan, who rule Homole's lovely plain,
deliver him unsued into my friend's hands!   110
—whether it be indeed the tender Philinus,
or whether another. Dear Pan, if you do so,
may the Arcadian boys never take squills
to your ribs and shoulders at times when meat is scarce.
But if otherwise, then be bitten all over your hide,
and scratch yourself with your nails: your bed be of nettles!
May the depths of winter find you among the mountains
of Thrace, turning beside the river Hebrus,
that lies toward the Pole; in summer may you
graze your herd a world away, among   120
the Ethiopians, under the Blemyes' rock,
whence Nile is no more seen. But you, O Loves,
with your apple blushes, leave the sweet vale
of Hyetis and Byblis, and Oecus, the steep seat
of blonde Dione, and strike me with your bows
the languorous Philinus, the wretch who nowise pities
my friend. And faith, he's already riper than a pear,
and the women cry, "Alas, your youthful flower
fades, Philinus!" Let us mount guard
over his threshold no more, Aratus: no more   130
wear out our feet, but let the morning's cockcrow
deliver another to numb grief! Let Molon
bear the bout and its punishment with, but we
find peace within, and an old witch beside
to spit on us, bidding all that is ugly avaunt.'

So much I spoke, and Lycidas, as before,
laughing merrily, made me accept his stick,
as a token of our friendship from the Muses,
and branching left, he went by the Pyxa road.
But Eucritus and I and pretty Amyntas turned   140

toward Phrasidamus' farm, and laid us down
on soft beds of scented rushes and new-stripped
vine leaves, while high overhead rustled
many a poplar and elm, and near at hand
from the nymphs' cave splashed the holy water.
On the shady boughs, the scorched cicadas carried
their chirping labour on, and the tree frog croaked
far off in the dense thorn brake. Larks and linnets
sang, and the turtledove made moan, and the bees
150 zoomed around and about the fountains. All things
smelt of a rich harvest and fruiting—abundance
of pears by our feet and apples rolled at our side,
and branches burdened with damsons earthward drooped.
A cask was loosed of the four-year seal on its head—
Ye nymphs of Castalia, dwelling on Parnassus' peak,
was it such a bowl that in Pholus' craggy cave
the aged Chiron placed before Heracles?
Such nectar persuaded the shepherd beside Anapus
dance among his pens—that strong Polyphemus
160 who pelted ships with mountains—such as you nymphs
set welling that day for our drink, beside the altar,
Demeter's, of the Threshing Floor? Ah, again
may I set up a great winnowing fan on her corn-heap
and she laugh, with sheaves and poppies in both her hands!

◈Idyll X

Alone among the bucolic Idylls this poem has an agricultural, not a pastoral theme. It is perhaps in keeping with this that it is also the most simply realistic, and that not only in point of character depiction, in which it may be compared with Idyll IV. Its double presentation of the situation of the lovelorn Boucaeus subjects Boucaeus' own account to the prismatic correction of an essentially prosaic character (for men of Milon's stamp there always is only one kind of poetry) so that it may be transmitted free from any distortions of an ailing fancy. Yet far as the poem is removed from idyllic idealizing, it is equally far from the 'realism' understood by our own age, which focusses on the debasing of human passions, which is rather the realism of Idyll V. In point of realism, then, it more closely resembles the mimes than the bucolic Idylls, and especially Idyll XIV, which deals twice with the same theme of lovesickness, that of Aeschinas for Cynisca and that of Cynisca for Lycus (the Woolf of my version). Comment passed on a distracted and unkempt lover's state, and on the absent cause of it, by a third party is a theme that is found in Callimachus, who uses it satirically, as well as Theocritus; it passes into Roman poetry as a commonplace (cf. Horace *Odes* I 27, Propertius I 9) and seems to derive from comedy. It has been observed that the symposium, or drinking party, is the appropriate mise-en-scène for these intimacies, and that its unexpected transference here to the cornfield would be savoured by the contemporary reader.* We are to recall that in Idyll III Theocritus has transferred the city practice of the *paraclausithuron* to the country, with risible effect, and if we accept this as a conscious device of Theocritus' art, we could even

*See Francis Cairns, 'Theocritus' Idyll x', *Hermes* 98 (1970):38–44.

suppose it symbolized in the citified boots of Simichidas, at which Lycidas mocks in Idyll VII, and indeed included in that Idyll's distinction of Theocritus' civic from his bucolic persona.

Idyll III also provides an instructive comparison with this poem in the matter of degrees of reality. There is the given situation: in X the beloved is no 'black browed nymph' dwelling in some cavern of romantic fantasy, but a farmer's slave girl whose thin figure and dark complexion are to the smitten Boucaeus charms additional to the musical talent from which, we infer, her master has named her Bombyca ('Piper'). In the eyes of Milon, who represents the point of view of the sane man, these are defects. Idyll III lacks this commentator figure (found also in XIV and IV), but there too the viewpoint of author and audience, which demarcates the fantasy world of III and the self-deception of X, emerges with the more or less deluded utterances of their lovelorn subjects. Idyll III we have already denoted grotesque on account of the 'credibility gap' between the goatherd's real situation and his fanciful self-projection. His soliloquy resolves aimlessly with a random hiss and spurt of emotion until he lies empty and prostrate, burnt out.

Turning to Boucaeus' song, we may perceive the distinction between the grotesque and the merely incongruous. Here the sentiments are set out in an orderly frame of reason and convention. Presumably the pragmatic Milon, in inviting Boucaeus to composition, has the healing effects of this ordering in view—comparable to the quasi-medicinal catharsis of song in Idyll XI. Only there is the ever-increasing twist of hyperbole to underscore Milon's viewpoint and to render the matter, to the audience, amusing. So the couplet in which the swarthy Bombyca is compared to dark flowers (a conceit which, like so many a Theocritean touch, recalls, in a general way, Shakespeare, so inveterate is the bucolic tradition) is followed by that in which the Greek commonplace of the eros drive in nature lapses into parody with the concluding image of the crane pursuing not the seed but the plough. There follows Boucaeus' socially outrageous ambition to offer up gold statues of Bombyca and himself in the temple of Aphrodite, which in its turn lapses into a bathetic concern to be portrayed in gentlemanly attire. His concluding attempt to present the physical charms of his mistress, in which truth—Milon's and the common view—holds the ascendant over his self-deception, is capped by Milon's ironical judgment on the performance as a whole. That Boucaeus' sentimentality is at all points patent and exposed renders it harmless and amusing. In Idyll III the goatherd's had a morbid, disturbing aspect.

Theocritus has scarcely been at pains to pinpoint the scene of this Idyll. Choice seems to lie between Sicily and Cos, and a number of oriental references may suggest the east rather than the west of the Mediterranean. 'Syrian' is an obvious example, particularly if it is a nickname, as my translation takes it to be. The western equivalent would more likely be 'Libyan' or more distantly, 'Ethiopian'. Then there is the name Polybotas, which in mythology is that of a giant felled by Poseidon with an up-torn portion of the island of Cos. Lityerses is known as the son of the legendary Midas, king of Phrygia. In the present context, he appears simply as patron of reapers and fount of their songs, and it may well be that his original and abiding popular association ends here. There is no hint of the sinister body of legend that attached to him, which indeed would detract from the healthy, suntanned manliness with which Milon aims to replace Boucaeus' infatuation, which he sees as jejune and fit only for milksops. We know that a type of reaping song was known as a *Lityersa* and emanated from Phrygia. No doubt Milon's Greek hexameter couplets are intended to represent this genre in a general manner through Theocritus' own formal medium, and not as imitations or quotations. A formal prayer to Demeter, goddess of the harvest, is followed by four agricultural maxims delivered in couplets, which have been compared to those of Hesiod's *Works and Days*.

In the concluding two couplets, Milon turns his attention to the wine and porridge provided for the reapers' midday meal, with gibes at the steward's meanness. This may suggest that the morning's reaping is drawing to a close, or more likely that their provender is a traditional theme for the songs of hearty reapers.

The Day Labourers

(Milon and Boucaeus)

MILON
Comrade Boucaeus, why are you acting so glum?
You're cutting a crooked swathe—it was straight enough
    once—
and not keeping up with your neighbour— lagging behind
like a sheep behind the flock, with a thorn in her foot!
Where will you be in the evening, or even at noonday
if right at the start you've not got your teeth in the row?

BOUCAEUS
Reapmaster Milon, chip of the tough old block!
Did you never experience grief for somebody absent?

MILON
Never. What business is that of a working man?

BOUCAEUS
10   You mean you've never spent sleepless nights for love?

MILON
I should hope not. Bad thing for a dog to taste tripe!

BOUCAEUS
Then let me tell you, I've been in love for ten days.

MILON
You draw on the barrel, it seems; I barely get lees!

BOUCAEUS
My kitchen garden's unhoed and all gone to seed.

MILON
Which of them's plaguing you?

BOUCAEUS
Polybotas' girl,
who piped to the reapers the other day at Hippocion's.

MILON
God finds out the sinner! You've got what you've asked for!
She'll cling to you o'nights like a mantis on a stalk!

BOUCAEUS
You're beginning to mock me—but not only Wealth is
    blind;
there's the wayward Eros as well, so mind your bluster!   20

MILON
I'll mind it. But you now lay your armful down
and strike up a tune—some love song to your mistress.
It sweetens toil, and you were a poet once.

BOUCAEUS (*sings*)
Pierian Muses, sing me the slender maid;
for all you goddesses touch is fairer made.

Charming Bombyca—called 'Syrian', maligned
as lean, and sallow; but I say 'olive-skinned'.

Is not the violet and the pictured iris black?
And yet in garlands must they never lack.

As goat on clover, wolf on goat, and crane   30
on plough is set, so I for you am fain.

Would I had all the wealth that Croesus had of old!
We'd lie before Aphrodite, the pair of us, in gold.

You with your pipes, an apple—perhaps a rose,
and I with proper sandals and smart clothes.

Charming Bombyca! Like knucklebones your feet,
A poppy of a voice—your airs I can't repeat!

MILON
Say, boys, Bouc never let on he could turn such verses!
How well he fitted the thing to the metre! Ah well,
40   I've been wasting my days, growing this old man's beard!
But hear these rhymes of the hero Lityerses.

(sings)
Demeter of the fruit and of the ear, bless this crop:
briskly be it harvested and bearing to the top!

Tighten your bundles, binders; let no one say
as he passes, 'Men of figwood! Wasted their pay!'

On the cut ends let the north and west winds blow;
you'll find the ears will fatten better so.

Let those who thresh the corn shun noonday rest,
for then the ear parts from the cornstalk best.

50   But let the reapers rise with the rising lark,
rest in the heat, and not leave off till dark.

A blessed life is the frog's, boys—what does he care
for the man who pours the drinks! His drink's right there!

Steward, your lentil mess is unbefitting;
you'll cut your stingy hand with cummin-splitting!

Those are the songs for men who work in the sun,
Boucaeus; your starveling love's a thing to tell
in your mother's ear, when she stirs in bed of a morning!

Idyll XI

The form of this poem, an epistle addressed to a friend of the author, links it with two others of the Idylls, VI to Aratus, and XIII to Theocritus' present correspondent, the doctor Nicias. Moreover, the three letters are all on the subject of love and convey advice by means of an illustrative story. Mention of Aratus is confined to the address by name; his name occurs again obliquely in Simichidas' song in Idyll VII, also in the context of advice on a love affair. Of Nicias we learn more from the opening lines of Idylls XI and XIII; in addition Idyll XXVIII and Epigram VIII concern him, and there is nothing conflicting in their account (see General Introduction, pp. 9–10). If his friendship with Theocritus dates from his days as a medical student (see General Introduction, p. 9) the common interest in love affairs is particularly understandable, as is also, in Idyll XI, Theocritus' assumption of 'experience' and in general the youthful tone of the opening and closing addresses to Nicias, whereas XIII speaks from a maturer standpoint. The closing line's gibe at Nicias' profession—an agelong theme found alike in Pindar and Chaucer, to omit more modern examples—also suggests the intimate terms of a youthful friendship, or of one originating in youth.

Nicias, as we learn from line 6, was also a poet. A Greek commentator informs us that he was a writer of epigrams and that he composed a reply to Theocritus, and quotes the opening lines. If these—a Homeric pastiche—are a fair sample of his work, or if the contemporary Nicias whose epigrams appear in Meleager's Garland is to be identified with him, his poetic talent was nothing outstanding. Here Theocritus uses it, together with Nicias' formal profession of doctor, to initiate the theme that the only remedy for love is poetic composition or song. There follows the illustrative account that forms the substance of Idyll

XI and also a link of another kind with Idyll VI: the tale of the Cyclops-shepherd Polyphemus, who loved to distraction the sea nymph Galatea. In Idyll VI, as has been seen, another aspect of the tale is used by the cowherds Daphnis and Damoetas to warn each other (and obliquely Aratus) to 'play it cool' in love (see the introduction to Idyll VI).

Both Idylls VI and XI, but especially the latter, exploit the Homeric background figure of the Cyclops. The adjective I have rendered 'in days of old', indeed, appears to introduce him; but lines 8–9 make it plain that we have here to do with this figure in his youth, his fate unknown to him (and not even foretold, as in Idyll VI) and yet in the audience's eyes upon him—as also, unconsciously, it is present in his own words at lines 50–51 and 58 (a reference to the *Odyssey*). The episode of the love of the Cyclops for Galatea is first found about 400 B.C. in a dithyrambic poet, Philoxenus of Cythera, and became a favourite subject for comedy. Callimachus also makes reference to it in an epigram addressed to a doctor, a curious fact which makes it seem likely he has Theocritus' Idyll in mind. The young Polyphemus as depicted by Theocritus is at times almost touchingly naive, a veritable bumpkin who appears unable to distinguish between the real Galatea and her appearances in his dreams (ll. 22–24), and at the same time intensely—we must suppose unselfconsciously—poetic, truly the archetypal figure for the bucolic idyll's comment on the human condition.* The overlaying of the Homeric ogre by the stripling Polyphemus, at grips with his threatened derangement, is a potent source of the poem's idiosyncratic, even audacious force.

A factor the importance of which has been overlooked is the traditional identity of Polyphemus' mother, a sea nymph named Thoösa. Here we may pause to admire the remarkably quasi-Freudian aspect of Theocritus' genius, for the sea origin of the mother accounts for the son's inevitable and immediate (l. 26) 'transference' to the sea nymph Galatea, which is moreover the

---

*This is well observed by E. W. Spoffard, 'Theocritus and Polyphemus', *American Journal of Philology* 90 (1969):22–35.

psychological significance of Thoösa's first bringing Galatea to him—a circumstance also dramatically appropriate, as Gow has noted. His sense of something in his inheritance essential to his happiness but which eludes him gives rise to the fanciful complaint about not having been born with gills (l. 52) and the desire to swim (l. 57). His mother did not pass on to him the physical apparatus necessary to fulfil the yearning for the sea that he inherited from her, and this is the real grudge against her which he rationalizes in line 65. That the Cyclops' unequal birth and resulting frustrations have wider 'metaphysical' indications for humanity in general (we are reminded of Caliban and of the whole 'sea change' motif of Shakespeare's *Tempest*) we expect from what has already been said about his archetypal bucolic role. How purely and universally archetypal he is may come as a surprise to those who regard the modern age as the first with any insight into psychodynamics. We are left with a final analyst's conundrum, which is also one about the degree of consciousness of the poet: are we to interpret Polyphemus' sea fixation as a mechanism enabling him to discount his physical hideousness, or is it rather that his sense of inferiority, focussing on his looks (a readily recognizable syndrome of adolescence) in fact relates to his 'crossed' origin? My answer is that Theocritus, acutely sensitive though he is to the psychological innuendos of myth and character, has not been led to pose the question so academically and simply presents us with a being who, himself symbolical, is a nice balance of related symbolisms.

The general theme of Idyll XI (found also in the treatment of Idyll VI), that of the literally earthbound mortal whose eros is directed toward a being of a superior order in nature, is also that of Idyll III, and it is interesting to compare the speakers in both poems. The Cyclops in fact exhibits a degree of psychic instability less extreme than that of the goatherd. His physical grotesqueness, and particularly his one eye, traditional since the *Odyssey*, is in the forefront of every reader's imagination from the moment his name is introduced. The snub nose and goatlike beard of the goatherd of Idyll III, over which he displays an excessive anxiety, are of Theocritus' own bestowal and so are sketched in early, his first appeal being against rejection on grounds of appearance. This self-consciousness indeed provides more than picturesque detail, for it is symptomatic of his general and oppressive sense of inferiority. Polyphemus too suffers from anxieties about being 'somebody', and 'noticed', as line 76 betrays, and the psychologically proper polarity of this syndrome is also present in the esteem he claims for himself as a man of property (ll. 33ff.). But the goatherd's inferiority complex gives rise to a far greater imbalance and violence of emotion than is depicted in Idyll XI, so that whereas Polyphemus reaches a similar nadir of depression, characterized by similar complaints of physical suffering, he is able to recognize the futility of despair and takes a sudden upward turn (at l. 69). The crisis is passed; the cathartic effect of song, if not quite preparing the triumph of self-determination, at least enables him to 'shepherd his love', bringing it within manageable proportions. The goatherd's song has no such effect, for it does not really refer to his situation or explore his passion, but merely aggrandizes it by a ludicrous comparison with the sufferings of lover-heroes. For him there is only the futility of self-pity dragged on to its end in nervous prostration.

On stylistic grounds it has been postulated that Polyphemus' song is an early composition later incorporated by Theocritus into his admonitory letter to Nicias. However, the apparent reference in Callimachus might suggest that the introductory passage is also fairly early. It would be attractive to hold that the modifications called for by a recension account for the abrupt transition at line 69—in which case the poem forms an interesting parallel with Idyll III, both being studies in the moral havoc precipitated by unequal love. But it is perhaps more likely that occasional verbal oddities are in fact an extra shaking of Sicilian Doric with which Theocritus has seasoned this uncouth shepherd of his native island, and that if anything is to be inferred from such a degree of metrical roughness as has been noticed, it has a similar function in displaying a somewhat rude poetic character. That it is a character far from entirely lacking in sensibility, the description of his early love bears witness in lines which inspired some famous ones of Virgil, who, however, transposes them to a setting altogether more decorous. The contrast serves to point out the characteristic boldness of Theocritus in so handling a bogey-figure of mythology as to illustrate at once the dignity and the repulsiveness of men.

The Cyclops

Love's a complaint, Nicias, against which no drug known
to Nature is effective: not an ointment, not a powder—
save for the Muses: through their art can men with this
    disease
be eased, and sweet relief they find—but few can find it.
And this I ween you know full well, being a physician,
and held in love exceeding by the selfsame Nine.
In days of old, my countryman, the Cyclops Polyphemus,
fared best with them, for one: he barely had a beard
on lip or cheek, when he fell in love with the sea nymph
    Galatea.

10 He wooed her, not with apples and roses and lovelocks,
but with so fine a frenzy that all beside seemed pointless.
Often enough his sheep had to find their own way home
to the fold from the green pastures, while he sang of
    Galatea,
sitting alone on the beach amid the sea wrack, languishing
from daybreak, with a deadly wound which mighty Cypris
dealt him with her arrow, fixing it under his heart.
Nevertheless, he found the cure, and seated high on a rock,
looking out to sea, this is how he would sing.

'O white Galatea, why do you spurn my love?

20 —whiter than curds to look on, softer than a lambkin,
more skittish than a calf, tarter than the swelling grape!
How do you walk this way, so soon as sweet sleep laps
    me,
and are gone as soon, whenever sweet sleep leaves me,
fleeing like a sheep when she spies the grey wolf coming!
I fell in love with you, maiden, the first time you came, with
    my mother,
eager to cull the bluebells from our hillside: I was your
    guide.
Once seen, I could not forget you, nor to this day can I yet;

not that you care: God knows you do not, not a whit!
O, I know, my beauty, the reason why you shun me:
the shaggy eyebrow that grins across my forehead,   30
unbroken, ear to ear; the one eye beneath;
and the nose squat over my lips. For all my looks,
I'd have you know, I graze a thousand sheep, and draw
the best milk for myself to drink. I am never without
cheeses, summer or fall: even in midwinter
my cheese nets are laden. There's not another Cyclops
can play the flute as I can, and I sing of you, my peach,
always of me and you, till dead of night, quite often.
I'm rearing eleven fawns, all with white collars,
for you, and four bear cubs. Come to us, then;   40
you'll lack for nothing. Leave the green sea gulping
against the dry shore. You'll do better o' nights with me,
in my cave; I've laurels there, and slender cypresses;
black ivy growing, and the honey-fruited vine;
and the water's fresh that tree-dressed Etna sends me,
a drink divine, distilled from pure white snow.
Who'd choose instead to stay in the salt sea waves?
And if my looks repel you, seeming over-shaggy,
I've heart of oak within, and under the ash a spark
that's never out. If you will fire me, gladly will I yield   50
my life, or my one eye, the most precious thing I have.
O, why did not my mother bring me to birth with gills!
Down I'd dive and kiss your hand—your lips if you'll
    allow—
and bring you white narcissus flowers, or soft poppies,
with wide, red petals—not both at the same time,
for one's, you see, a winter, the other a summer flower.
Even so, sweetheart, I've made a start: I'm going to learn
    to swim,
if some stranger comes this way, sailing in a ship,
and find out why it is you nymphs like living in the deep.
O, won't you come out, Galatea, and coming out forget,   60
as I, as I sit here, forget to go back home!
You'd learn to like to shepherd sheep with me, and milk,

and set the curds for cheese, dropping in sharp rennet.
Only my mother does me wrong, and it's her I blame.
She's never said a single word on my behalf to you,
for all she sees me growing thin, day after day.
I shall tell her that my head and both my feet are throbbing:
so I'll be even, making her suffer, even as she makes me.
Cyclops, Cyclops! Where is this mad flight taking you?
You'd surely show more sense if you'd keep at your basket
70   weaving,
and go gather the olive shoots and give them to the lambs.
Milk the ewe that's at hand: why chase the ram that's
    fleeing?
Perhaps you'll find another Galatea, and more fair.
Many a girlie calls me out to play with her by night,
and when I do their bidding, don't they giggle gleefully!
I too am clearly somebody, and noticed—on dry land!'

In this way did Polyphemus shepherd his love with song;
and he found a readier cure than if he had paid hard cash.

☙Idyll XII

Suspicion has been cast on the authenticity of this poem, chiefly because alone in the Theocritean collection it is written in the Ionic dialect. But even apart from the fact that the tradition as to Theocritus' authorship is as good for this as for any other poem in the corpus—it is in the earliest manuscript, the Antinoan papyrus of ca. 500 A.D.—there is no reason to suppose that a poet who amply demonstrates his virtuosity in different dialects (see General Introduction, p. 17) should not at some time have tried his hand at the Ionic. True, his other surviving love poems (Idylls XXIX, XXX, and the hopelessly fragmentary XXXI) are in the speech of Sappho and Alcaeus, and also in Sapphic metres, whereas the present poem is in hexameters. They, however, are on internal evidence products of his maturer years, whereas other considerations, besides those of metre and dialect, suggest that Idyll XII is a relatively early work. While these other Idylls display the disillusion of experience, the dominant mood here is of a scarcely inhibited optimism. There is, moreover, a certain crudity in the poem's transitions, though, as I purpose to show, far slighter than has been supposed, and certainly not enough to impugn its authenticity, since once a coherent approach to interpretation is made the poem will be found to be extremely characteristic of our author.

The failures of interpretation that have bedeviled the poem's appraisal are perhaps not to be wondered at, since the scholarly eye is more adapted to fixing itself on detail than to following up with the comprehensive view necessary to literary criticism. To the analytic scrutiny—certainly a preliminary *sine qua non*— the opening emotional pitch is lost in a string of conventional comparisons and is artificially resuscitated for the central passage of prophecy and prayer—only to be let go again in favour of an annoyingly Alexandrian display of pedantry by the dragging in of recherché words for 'lover' and 'beloved'. We have granted a measure of roughness in these transitions compatible with poetic immaturity, but for one who grasps the significance of the opening and enters into the poem aware that it is a *dramatic representation* of the author 'surprised by joy', the following series of literary comparisons will fulfil their function of providing space —a plateau, as it were—for the author's (and reader's) rapt contemplation of his beatitude. The rhythm, with the enjambement throwing the emphasis on 'sweeter', is, in the Greek at least, excellently contrived to sustain the euphoria induced by the boy's sudden appearing, and the slight logical irregularity in the comparison, when it emerges, only assists the effect. In the case of the second 'interruption', the linguistic lore makes the legitimate dramatic contribution of evoking the 'all manner of men' to whom the lovers will become a legend.

No less a stumbling block to the proper appraisal of this poem has been the concluding passage. Evoked here is an otherwise unknown kissing contest at a (known) festival at Megara in honour of one Diocles, who according to the legend fled from Attica and was killed in battle while defending his boy-love. It has been claimed that if ever so bizarre a custom as the kissing contest existed and survived into so sophisticated an age, it could hardly have been meant to be taken seriously by Theocritus' contemporary audience.* The conclusion is that it is a jest, which leaves the alternatives that the poem's ending forms yet another and more jarring discord, or that the whole should be regarded as a burlesque—an interpretation which squares particularly ill with the dominant tone of exaltation induced by love returned. This clearly will not do, nor does Gow seem to offer the clue to more than the external wrappings of the enigma when he writes that 'it may be that if we knew the models which dictated this choice [of Ionic hexameters] we should under-

*By Wilamowitz, discussed in A. S. F. Gow, *Theocritus: Edited with a Translation and Commentary*, Vol. 2, *Commentary, Appendix, Indexes, and Plates* (Cambridge: At the University Press, 1952) [hereinafter referred to as Gow], p. 221.

stand also what at present seem incongruities in the poem.'* If Theocritus is the author—and inevitably one way of sidestepping the issue has been to infer that he is not—then we are right to expect that sure appeal to universal human responses which is elsewhere his hallmark, as it is almost the definition of artistic genius of whatever cultural origin. The following schematic interpretation starts from a reliance on the evidence that this is a genuine work of our author, and claims, as it were by a correction of focus, to restore the work to a unity of content, mood, and style adequate not to disgrace or belie this origin. It is expected that further refinement may be possible along the lines of interpretation indicated, in the light of new knowledge.

Theocritus joyfully greets a boy whose spontaneous return to him after two days' absence is an unlooked-for sign of his attachment. His appearance is like the dawn with which he comes, rejuvenating one to whom his absence has seemed a lifetime of longing. After the opening apostrophe of surprise and welcome, action is suspended for five lines, during which the poet appears as though accrediting his eyesight and taking stock of the measure of his happiness. Then he rushes into his arms 'as a sunscorched traveler runs to the shade of an oak tree'. With delight it dawns on him that the boy returns his love (Gow points out that 'in this relationship the affections of the man are usually more deeply engaged than those of the boy', and this consideration explains why the boy is said to 'reward twofold' at line 27) and he is moved to hope for the smooth course of a perfect love match henceforth. His imagination is roused: they will be a legend and a model to coming generations. He projects the things that will be said of them by the mouths of Greeks of differing speech. (That this is the dramatic justification of the display of linguistic curiosities here is borne out by the expression 'in the mouths of all' in line 22.) The prophetic vision culminates in a prayer that it may be so, and that he, long gone from this life, may in the Underworld receive reports of this undying fame. But he turns from his imaginings, leaving the future to the gods.

*Gow, p. 221.

Enough now to praise his beloved, for no eventualities can give the lie to the present bliss he brings. Here, with his descent from airy castle-building, enters the first intimation of the doubt that lingers beyond the concluding lines of the poem.

The following couplet is central to the interpretation, since it reinforces what could only be inferred from the opening couplet: that the anguish experienced by Theocritus during the two days of darkness and the powerful upsurge of joy as the reality of the boy's return, and its implications for a mutual eros, dawns on him, are explicable not by a mere separation but by a bitterness —the boy had taken advantage of his position to wound his lover. Yielding to the intoxication of the present and his beloved's embrace, the poet's thoughts drift to kisses given and received at a festival which gives public and religious recognition to such bliss as his—a touch surely of the same hand that depicted the trancelike state of Simaetha in Idyll II (see the introduction to Idyll II). He blesses the felicity of the judge whose mouth can discriminate between kisses true and false—and with this reminder that kisses may be false ends a poem worthy of Theocritus' psychological mastery and self-knowledge. If jest there be, it is on a secondary level: no mere ridicule but the sad, wry smile of retrospection as the poet recreates the emotion that overwhelmed him in that hour, and allows us to glimpse the veiled doubt that haunts even the utmost felicity of the lover.

To the Harkener

Dear boy, you have come, as the third day draws
to dawn, but those who desire, in a day they grow old!
By as much as the spring surpasses the summer, as apples
are sweeter than sloes, fleecier ewe than her lamb;
by as much as a maid o'ermatches a thrice-wed wife,
and kid than calf is nimbler, the clear-tongued nightingale
most musical of all birds, by so much your appearing
has cheered me, and I have run to you as a traveller
runs from the scorching sun to an oak tree's shade.
Would equal Loves might breathe upon us both,   10
and we a legend be to all posterity:
'Among our forebears came, most like to gods,
two mortal men—"Inspirer" say the Spartans;
the other, too, Thessalians call the "Harkener".
Yoke-mates they were, in love. Yea, in those days
of old were men of gold, when the beloved
loved in return!' Father Zeus, and you unaging
immortals, would that this might be, and one
two hundred generations hence might stand
at Acheron's one-way gate, to me announcing: 20
'The love between you and your gracious Harkener
is in the mouths of all, the young especially!'
These things the heavenly gods must oversee;
it shall be as they will. But if I praise you,
no liar's warts shall sprout on my slight nose.
For though you leave a smart, you heal directly,
reward twofold—I go with hands o'erladen.
Megarians of Nisaea, you who excel at rowing,
prosperous may you live, for you honoured beyond all
   others
the Attic stranger, Diocles, boy-lover.   30
Ever about his tomb, in early spring,
a throng of youths contend for the prize at kissing:
whoever more sweetly presses lips to lips

returns to his mother laden with garlands. Happy
who judges between the boys' kisses. Surely
he bright-eyed Ganymede plies with prayers
for a mouth like the Lydian touchstone, wherewith gold
is told by the moneychangers, true from false.

✤Idyll XIII

This poem is justly famed for the sustained beauty of its lines and the wistful delicacy with which is retold an old tale of love and loss—the rape of Hylas. Several passages reveal the author's delight in the observation of natural beauty: the passing description of the mother hen calling her chicks to roost; the flight of the *Argo*, 'like an eagle' into the Euxine (Black Sea); the sight of her first harbourage in the Propontis (Sea of Marmara); and most particularly the evocation of the spring to which Hylas comes to draw water, with its natural and supernatural life: the 'inscape' of the wild plants that grow beside it yielding place in the narrative to the patterned dance of its familiar nymphs and their melodious names.

The poem has a peculiar literary–historical interest, since it bears resemblances too marked to be accidental to the Hylas episode in the *Argonautica* of Theocritus' contemporary, Apollonius of Rhodes (see the introduction to Idyll VII). This monumental epic relates the hero Jason's quest of the Golden Fleece and is our chief source for this body of myth, which it narrates at length in all its ramifications and with many a learned digression. The material was produced by the Greek fantasy's penetrating a space as daunting and challenging as any in modern fiction—that lying beyond the eastern confines of the Mediterranean. Its westward counterpart is the *Odyssey*. A specimen adventure gets a passing reference in the present poem: the feat of the hero ship *Argo*—itself quasi-personified—in passing between the Symplegades (the 'Clashing Rocks'), the gateway to the Euxine imaginatively conceived. The Symplegades mark the eastward limit of the *terra cognita* of the Greeks, just as the Pillars of Hercules (the Straits of Gilbraltar) mark the westward. The incident is alluded to here for its value in establishing scene and epic atmosphere. The actual tragedy of Heracles and Hylas takes place west of the Euxine, and therefore prior to this, on the southern shore of the partly-known Propontis, in the land of the Ciani, more commonly known as Bithynia.

Theocritus' 'Hylas' is an 'epyllion', an epic in miniature, as are also his 'Dioscuri' and 'Baby Heracles' (see the introductions to Idylls XXII and XXIV). In keeping with this is the choice of style and language, which is more heavily larded with Homerisms than is usual with Theocritus (cf. General Introduction p. 17). Instances are numerous but among them may be cited the epithetic phrases: 'white-armed Dawn', 'wealthy Iolcus', 'hollow *Argo*', 'fair-haired Hylas', 'steadfast Telamon', and others that imitate (or are) stock Homeric epithets; also the heroic similes of the falling star and the ravening lion; and the passages characterizing season and hour—the time of the *Argo*'s sailing and the evening, when the chickens go to roost. This last passage, contrasting oddly though it does with the preceding stereotype of the dawn, evokes the *megaron*, the great hall common to men and animals, which is the central feature of the Homeric manor house. This very love of including homely and intimate detail within the epic's grander scope is a Homeric (and un-Apollonian) trait. It is frequently found in the *Odyssey*, particularly in the characterization of Helen at Menelaus' palace in Sparta. A famous example in the *Iliad* is the account of Hector's leave-taking of his wife, when their child is frightened by the plume on his helmet; we may compare Theocritus' description of Alcmene putting her babies to bed, in Idyll XXIV. In this appreciation of the beauties of everyday life, Theocritus could certainly claim to be more Homeric than his rival, Apollonius.

It has been disputed whose account of the Hylas story is prior. The evidence is in favour of Theocritus' being a deliberate correction of Apollonius' since it is at key points of divergence superior in taste and style.* The same holds true for the first part of Idyll XXII, where Theocritus recasts the episode that in Apol-

---

*See Gow, pp. 231–32. For a contrary, though to my mind unconvincing interpretation, see A. Köhnken, *Apollonios Rhodios und Theokrit*, Hypomnemata, vol. 12 (Goettingen: Vandenhoeck and Ruprecht, 1965), *passim*.

lonius follows hard upon that of Hylas: the encounter of the Dioscuri with Amycus, king of the Bebryces. In the case of Hylas, the decisive factor is that Theocritus supplies the needed psychological motivation for Heracles' distracted conduct. Apollonius makes no mention of a love relationship; for him, Hylas is simply Heracles' captive servant boy. If he had had Theocritus' dramatically far finer account before him, he could hardly have challenged comparison while omitting this aspect of the original.

In Theocritus' poem, the love motive is essential to theme as well as integral to plot, for the professed purpose of the poem is to give another admonition to Nicias, who is still, it seems, in the toils of Eros. As in Idyll XI, it is likely that the address to his friend is no more than a pretext for the presentation of material of independent origin, in the present case having perhaps an ulterior purpose, namely that Nicias, being himself a poet, would appreciate its quality and the literary point it is making. The overt lesson is characteristic: we aggrandize ourselves and our own affairs; we should recall that we are but mortals; there were before us supermen such as Heracles (the epic epithet 'bronze-hearted' may denote both strength and immortality) who were subdued by the love god. Previously it had been 'poetry is the remedy for love'; here it is 'other and better men have suffered a like slavery'—both lessons no doubt readily applicable to Nicias' entanglement. It is noteworthy that in both poems the culprit god Eros is demythologized, as is fitting between gentlemen of science: in Idyll XI he is a disorder; here he is an 'inward god' who 'gnaws at the liver' (the literal sense of the Greek). The epithet 'cruel', however, recalls the roles of Eros in Idylls I and II and the 'thug of a god' (more literally, 'heavy god') in Idyll III. And those afflicted by him are perverse, 'stubborn' (see l. 70).

The theme is by now familiar, but whereas in Idyll XI it was applied to the anti-heroic Polyphemus (and that in the days of his nonentity) and in Idyll I to the rustic hero Daphnis, here Theocritus' purpose requires that it be demonstrated of a great hero. However, we must notice that Heracles, though one of the most popular figures of Greek mythology, is not a Homeric hero, and that as happens with legendary figures whose chief attributes are superhuman strength and appetite, he has an abiding tendency towards the buffoon, which accounts for his frequent appearances in satyr plays and comedies as well as in tragedies. Perhaps we may say that it is this very versatility of the whole man writ large which makes him a fitting figure for Theocritus' purposes here. Both his heroic attributes and his buffoonery can be exploited in a poem showing the degeneration of the hero under the power of love. For apart from the incongruity of the superman—whose natural companion is 'steadfast Telamon' (l. 43)—in love with the girlish Hylas ('of the flowing hair', l. 8),[*] whom he fondly hopes to turn into a man of his own stature (ll. 10ff.: a sense suggested by the imperfect tense of the Greek verb), there is the indignity of rage at his loss, which appears in his uncontrolled snatching up of weapons and bellowing the name of Hylas, and ends by driving him in frenzy over rough and trackless countryside. In the simile of the lion and the kid with which the account climaxes, we must surely read, besides the incongruity and the rage, something more bestial, since Hylas, the beloved, here appears as the prey. The penultimate two lines of the poem depict Heracles' companions calling his manhood in question with a play on words which I have attempted to render by 'heroes . . . our hero' (l. 78). Not until Heracles has completed on foot the long and purgatorial journey referred to in the final line, and has rejoined the Argonauts at Colchis, is he readmitted among the heroes.

Thus we have considered the separate literary and epistolary characters of this Idyll, and the former has appeared integral to its purpose, the latter adventitious. Of least moment is its character as cult-commemorative literature, but this perhaps deserves a passing mention. That there was an ancient cult of Hylas we know, and further that a feature of its liturgy was the threefold calling on his name. It would seem that Heracles'

*Noted by D. J. Mastronarde, 'Theocritus' Idyll 13: Love and Hero', *Parola del Passato* 23 (1968):6ff., and *Transactions of the American Philological Association* 99 (1968):275ff.

thrice-repeated cry of 'Hylas' refers to this one item. The inferring of *aitia*, or origins of ritual, was a sport dear to Hellenistic writers and not least Apollonius, who however failed to make capital of this one, perhaps because he was intent on another that involved the introduction at this point of the extraneous and superfluous figure of Polyphemus. It is at least unconscious irony on Theocritus' part that in excising Apollonius' *aition* he substituted another of which the propriety and artistic value cannot be called in question.

Hylas

Who of gods soever, Nicias, he was,
the sire of Eros did not have us in view
alone, though once we thought so. We were not
the first to whom fair seemed fair, who go
with hearts of flesh and do not see the morrow.
The bronze-hearted son of Amphitryon, too,
who withstood the savage lion, loved a boy,
the graceful Hylas with the flowing hair,
and taught him all, as a father his own son,
10   the lore that to himself was virtue and renown.
Formed to his own ideal the boy should be,
and draw in the same yoke with him till manhood.
They were never apart, not when the noon was high;
not when the white-armed Dawn went running up
to her father's house; not when the chicks looked up
cheeping to their roost, when the mother hen
flapped her wings, high on a smoky rafter.
And so, when Aeson's son went sailing after
the Golden Fleece—Jason, whom heroes followed
20   from all the cities, all who had any worth—
then went the man of suffering, son of Alcmene,
princess of Midea, down to wealthy Iolcus;
and Hylas went down with him into *Argo*
of the strong thwarts—the ship that did not so much
as graze the sombre Clashing Rocks, but sped
between, like an eagle, into the great gulf,
and ran straight on for the deep river Phasis,
leaving them standing, reefs until this day.
At the time of year when the Pleiads rise in the morning,
30   and the young lambs are turned to graze on the hillsides,
and spring becomes summer, the picked band of heroes
remembered their voyage, and taking their place in *Argo*'s
womb, they came with the wind on the third day
to the Hellespont, and anchored in the Propontis.

Where the Cian oxen draw the broad share
over the ploughland, there they disbarked at evening,
and two by two, on the beach, concocted a meal.
A meadow lay to their hand, royally stocked
with bedstraw: bullrush blades they cut, and dense
galingale, and put together one bivouac.   40
And bright-haired Hylas took a brass pitcher
and went in search of water for their supper,
for Heracles himself and steadfast Telamon,
who were comrades in arms and messmates. He soon
    discovered
a spring in a low-lying spot, thick with rushes,
with lustrous kingcups, pallid maidenhair,
swelling celery, and coarse marsh grasses.
In the deep of the pool, three nymphs threaded their
    dance—
the unsleeping nymphs, dread of the countryside—
Eunice and Malis, and Nycheia with spring in her glances.   50
Intent on filling his thirsty pitcher, he lowered it
close to the surface, and they laid hands on him, all
by Eros fancy-struck for the Argive boy.
Headlong he fell, under the black water,
as a flaming star falls headlong under the sea.
(And some sailor, seeing it, says to his mates,
'lighten the tackle, boys; the wind sits fair.')
The nymphs were trying to soothe the weeping boy
with gentle words, holding him on their laps.
But Amphitryon's son grew anxious; took up the club   60
that was never far from his hand and went in search.
Three times, as loud as his vast throat could vent,
he roared the name of Hylas; three times the boy
gave answer; his voice rose faint from the water
and sounded far, though he was close at hand.
At the bleat of a kid in the mountains, a hungry lion
springs from his couch to seize the ready prey:
so was Heracles driven on by his passion,
this way and that, among the trackless thorns,

70   over a deal of ground. Such the stubbornness
     of lovers, that he could toil so over bush
     and mountain! Jason's affairs went all unheeded.
     The ship stood under sail, her crew aboard;
     at night the heroes lowered the tackle, waiting
     for Heracles. Frenzied he followed wherever his feet
     led, for a cruel god gnawed at his vitals.
     And that is how Hylas the Beautiful joined the Bless'd,
     and how the heroes came to taunt our hero
     for skipping ship, that he left the thirty-thwarted
80   *Argo* short of an oar, and came on foot
     to the Colchians' land and the surly gulf of Phasis.

✿Idyll XIV

The Greek mime, to which classification Idylls XIV and XV are normally (and fairly) assigned, has been delineated in the General Introduction, where the relationship to this category of Idylls II and X (a transitional piece) has also been discussed. Another link between Idylls XIV and X was noticed in the introduction to the latter: they share the theme of the interrogation of a lover and the proffering of comment and advice on his affair and its object, which is also found in Callimachus and by Augustan times, at least, has become a recognizable poetic type.* In the present Idyll, the theme is found twice over, in the opening questioning of Aeschinas by Thyonichus, and in the questioning of Cynisca at the drinking party.

If character is necessarily the stuff of mime (as of comedy), this is particularly true of Theocritus, who uses the mime as he uses the pastoral idyll, to explore the dynamism of human behaviour as it relates to different situations. His characters, drawn with a loving closeness foreign to Herondas (see p. 16), invite, and repay, inspection. We will begin with the protagonist.

Aeschinas is early revealed by his old friend Thyonichus to be 'peppery [literally 'sharp']—liking things to your turn'—that is, ill-tempered and exigent ('of choleric humour', as the Elizabethans would put it). That he is demanding is again intimated towards the end, in Thyonichus' caution on dealings with Ptolemy. And Thyonichus 'knows' him, as Aeschinas himself tells us in shamefaced half-admission of his brutality towards Cynisca, his erstwhile mistress, excusing his fisticuff attack on her—which makes the audience well understand her preference for another! Clearly one thing Aeschinas is always demanding and unable to

*See Cairns, 'Theocritus' Idyll X', pp. 38–40.

do without is his woman. The reference to the mouse who tasted pitch appears to be proverbial for an addiction. We find the same language of remedy and cure as in Idyll XI—only here, Aeschinas being no poet, the erotic 'disease' is unpretentiously crude. Once again, Theocritus displays his hallmark—his fascination by the psychology of Eros. (How he would have approved Freud's thesis that psychic energy in effect *is* Eros!)

That Thyonichus 'knows' his friend's amorousness as well as his hot temper appears from his opening ironic query as to the latter's 'preoccupation' (the Greek word means both 'concern' and the object of concern or 'darling'). There is a further 'knowing' hint in the jesting reference to his curls—the dandy's lovelocks. It is clear both here and in Aeschinas' own reference to his 'Thracian haircut' (the precise point is lost on us) that his hair is unkempt on head and face. His moustaches straggle—implying also (at this period) a beard, which in itself had become an uncouth item since Alexander the Great set the fashion of shaving. Of a piece is his racy narrative, further enlivened by proverbial allusions—the mouse, the bull who made off to the woods (apparently the opening of a fable), and the 'sorry Megarians'. These are said to have asked the oracle at Delphi who were the greatest of the Greeks and been told to their discomfiture they were 'neither third nor fourth nor twelfth nor accounted nor in the reckoning'. Aeschinas, as appears, is a countryman, and something of a buffoon—as we already sense from the opening jocular greeting to his friend.

Thyonichus is conceived primarily as a foil and confidant for Aeschinas and as a mouthpiece for the manifesto on behalf of service with Ptolemy II. He regards his friend with amused detachment, greeting and condoling with him in formal terms, rallying him on his spleenful and amorous disposition. His view of the soldier's trade is a detached 'take it if you've a stomach for it', and his account of Ptolemy—while obviously conveying the poet's compliments—has the semblance of objectivity. In keeping with his cool character is the sententious utterance on age that closes the poem.

Then there is Cynisca. The name means 'little bitch' and may have been chosen by Theocritus as appropriate to her role, depending as it does on being some man's pet and pastime. Cynisca (in its Greek form *Kuniska*) recalls Kunna, a name given to prostitutes and having its (also abused) English cognate. However, the name Cynisca must have had respectable associations, since a daughter of the fifth-century King Agis of Sparta is known to have borne it.

That Cynisca is a hetaira is clear from her relationship to Aeschinas. As such, she takes her place at the men's meal, where she sits on a stool while they recline. The Greek word *hetaira*, which means 'companion', was used of a broad class of women ranging from the trollop to the salon-lady or bluestocking. What they had in common was their lack of married status and consequent need of male protection and support. In return for this they gave their 'companionship', which could, as famous hetairas from Pericles' Aspasia to the Epicurean Leontion demonstrate, confer benefits beyond merely physical intercourse. Cynisca appears to fit somewhere in the middle of the spectrum. Certainly she is no 'casual'; she has attached herself to one man and exercises her preference in leaving him for another. Equally certainly she has little in the way of cultural pretensions, or she would have had no truck with the boorish Aeschinas. Probably Labes' son is a cut above Aeschinas in status as well as in manners. He is at all events young and personable and in this contrasts with our honest knight—a fact which, we may infer, exacerbates the latter's jealous rage, so that he loses control of himself, thereby, and realistically, underscoring the comparison in his disfavour!

In all three mimes, Theocritus displays a notable sympathy for womankind, and particularly for the socially unprotected women, Simaetha and Cynisca, both impelled by their situation to seek out a man and cast themselves on his mercy. Simaetha is not a hetaira, but in following her preference she is attracted to the playboy Delphis, who never envisages making her his legal wife, so we may fairly assign her to the type and predict, if we will, her future gravitation towards it. Although the mood of the present poem is prevailingly humorous, Aeschinas stands condemned for his intolerance and brutality, as does Delphis for his lightness—and both betray what Shakespeare might have called their coxcombry—the male's swaggering self-interest and carelessness of the woman. Aeschinas means his remark about the 'six-year-old' in a contemptuous sense, and yet ironically it conveys, together with his own insensitivity, his 'maker's' tenderness—seen also in Simaetha's reference to sleeping children, and in the portrayal of Alcmene in Idyll XXIV. In this passing picture of the girl child crying until set upon her mother's lap—the closeness of two female beings in a male world—we note again Theocritus' love of intimate everyday detail which, in the introduction to Idyll XIII, we have compared to Homer. Indeed, Homer's influence here is plainly to be found—but with a significant modification. For in Book XVI of the *Iliad*, it is Patroclus who cries 'like a little girl who runs to her mother and demands to be taken up, clinging to her skirt and dragging her back as she walks, weeping and raising her eyes to be taken up'.* The criticism conveyed there is on two counts: puerility and effeminacy; but if Cynisca is charged with behaving like a child, the reader exonerates her, sensing that she has been put in the child's position—bullied by a 'larger' figure and never allowed to grow up. And even in his bluster, Aeschinas by this image reveals latent kinder feelings, as also by that of the swallow, in which he describes Cynisca catching up her skirts and fleeing from the house, where the association of tenderness is the whole reason for the particularization of the bird's motive for flying out from under the eaves: otherwise it is hardly appropriate, nor would Theocritus' fondness for the maternal behaviour of birds (cf. Idyll XIII) excuse its intrusion.

These passages are so reminiscent of each other that they might almost seem to suggest that the traditional placing of the mime (Idyll XIV) after the epyllion (XIII) authentically reflects their closeness in time of composition. On the other hand, Idyll XIII is usually conjoined with Idyll XI, which is regarded as an early work, and Idyll XIV assigned to the period of the other Idylls connected with Egypt and Ptolemy: the formal encomium

*Cited by Gow, p. 253.

(XVII) and the Alexandrian mime (XV). To the latter, on account of its comparable form and tone, the present poem is wont to be considered a (slighter) companion piece. But when all is said, we lack evidence as to date. Clearly this Idyll was composed during the reign of Ptolemy II, but that extended over thirty-seven years (283–246 B.C.). In the case of Idyll XV, greater precision can be reached from the allusions to Ptolemy's sister-consort Arsinoë II, but no 'argument from silence' applies to Idyll XIV, since the poem provides no good reason why she should be mentioned even if it was composed during her reign (275–270 B.C.). Nor will the contention hold that Theocritus would not during this period have described Ptolemy as a 'ladies man' (Greek *erōtikos*), since Ptolemy himself by no means treated his amours as a subject for reticence but on the contrary publicly commemorated his many mistresses with monuments.* Nor yet can we connect recommendation of service under the monarch with the war between Egypt and Syria (276–73 B.C.) or any other war, since the remark does not seem intended to procure recruits for Ptolemy's army so much as royal cognizance of its author's expressions of loyalty. Ptolemy is praised not specifically for his excellence as a warlord but generally for his princely character. This could equally well represent the flattery of a poet receiving patronage or an attention-getting ploy preliminary to the main assault of Idyll XVII (see General Introduction). The latter hypothesis would place Idyll XIV before 273 B.C.; the former between 273 and 270 B.C. Moreover, it seems likely (but cf. p. 10) that the observation that Ptolemy was one to know his enemy still better than his friend was intended as compliment and not—as it must have appeared after Theocritus' withdrawal from Alexandria— as a rueful reflection on his experience at close quarters. Theocritus—as Idyll XVII reveals him to us—was hardly the man to invite that sort of attention.

*See Gow's comments on dating, p. 246.

Aeschinas and Thyonichus

AESCHINAS
Good morrow to my lord Thyonichus!
     THYONICHUS And the same to you, Aeschinas!
It's been a long time.
     AESCHINAS It has.
        THYONICHUS What's your preoccupation?

AESCHINAS
I'm not doing too well, Thyonichus.
     THYONICHUS So I noticed.
You're thin, and all this moustache, and straggly locks—
reminds me of the Pythagorist who turned up the other
    day—
pale face, bare feet—said he was an Athenian.

AESCHINAS
Was he lovesick, too?
           THYONICHUS I should think so—for
    wheaten bread!

AESCHINAS
You will have your joke, sir; as for me, Cynisca—
the witch—is playing me up, and before I know it
10   I'll be out of my mind—I'm a hair's breadth off as it is!

THYONICHUS
That's so like you, old man; you're a wee bit peppery;
you want everything to your turn; but tell me the latest.

AESCHINAS
Well, I and the Argive, and the horsey fellow from
    Thessaly,
Agis, and the mercenary, Cleonicus, were drinking in the
    country,

near my place. I'd slaughtered a couple of fowls
and a sucking pig, and I opened some Biblian for them—
four years old, and a bouquet almost as fresh
as the day it was pressed! Plus the odd shallot
and snails I produced—it was a merry party.
Things were in full swing, when we voted to pledge   20
each one's toast in the neat—he must only say who.
Every one called, and we drank the toasts, as agreed.
Only she had said nothing, though I was by.
Can you imagine my feelings? 'Won't you call?
Seen a wolf, have you?' asked someone in jest.
'How clever you are,' says she, and she flamed up so,
you might have easily taken a light for a lamp!
It is Woolf! Woolf! My neighbour Labes' son!
He's tall and supple, and many say he's handsome.
This was the wonderful passion was burning her up!   30
I had caught some whispered word of it in the past,
but I never followed it up—beshrew this beard!
Much good it's done me to grow to manhood!
By now the four of us were deep in our cups,
and Agis set himself to sing 'My Wolf'—
a Thessalian catch—they're devils all! So Cynisca
bursts into hotter tears than a six-year-old
cries for her mammy to take her in her lap!
Then I—you know me, Thyonichus—dotted her one
with a right to the temple, and followed it up with the left.   40
She caught up her skirts and speeded out of the room.
'So I don't please you, Madam Pox that you are to me!
You're cuddling something prettier, are you? Then go,
and warm your other flame! Are your tears for him?
Then let them flow like—apples!' She flew then, fairly!
A swallow with nestlings under the eaves will give them
a tit-bit and dart off again to collect another;
Cynisca was swifter than that, off her hassock and through
the vestibule and the gates—just followed her feet!
'A bull made off for the woods', the fable goes. . . .   50

Twenty days . . . add eight . . . nine . . . ten . . . Ten more,
plus eleven, brings us to today, and two days more
makes two months since we parted—and whether I'm
   wearing
a Thracian haircut, she hasn't cared to find out!
Now Woolf is all. To Woolf her door is open
even at night, and we are not thought worthy
a single word—simply not in the reckoning—
'Sorry Megarians, least esteem their portion'.
If I only could fall out of love—everything else
60   would fall into place. But how? I'm like the mouse
who tasted pitch—you know the rest, Thyonichus—
and what the cure for hapless love may be,
I know not—except that Simus, after he fell
for that brazen baggage, went to sea and returned
heart-whole, and he was my age. I too
would sail the seas. Your soldier's not the first
of men, perhaps, but nor is he the worst;
let's say a fair average.
              THYONICHUS Aeschinas,
I wish your fortunes had squared with your desires;
70   but if, as you say, you've a mind to go abroad,
the best of paymasters for a free man is Ptolemy.

AESCHINAS
And in other ways, what sort of man is he?

THYONICHUS
All in all, the best: beneficent, cultured,
a ladies' man, a courtier bred to the bone;
knows his friend, his enemy even better;
ample in his favours, and, as becomes a king,
refuses nothing he's asked for—only remember,
Aeschinas, it doesn't do to be always asking!
So, if you've a fancy to clasp your cloak's tail

on your right shoulder, and on your two feet stand   80
your opposite number's onslaught—off to Egypt!
We grow old from the temples up, and all the while
hoary Time keeps stealing down your cheeks!
While there's sap in the joints, we must be stirring.

❧Idyll XV

In the garden of human wit the comedy of bourgeois domesticity appears as a hardy perennial. Idyll XV therefore needs little elucidation. In commenting on Idylls II and XIV we have observed Theocritus' gift of insight into feminine character. There women of the hetaira type were in question (see the introduction to Idyll XIV). Where the present sketch is concerned, pathos has been bowed out by the assigning of a socially secure station to the protagonists, who are two married women—but sympathetic insight, here directed onto their limited everyday lives, is, for all the lighthearted garb it wears, as active as ever in Theocritus.

The name Praxinoa may be Englished as 'Busy-mind', and her slave Eunoa's, by contrast, as 'Well-intentioned' (with, like the Greek *euēthēs*, something of the condescension often carried by 'innocent' or the old senses of 'silly' and 'simple'). Gorgo is a fairly common name and, while such a libel can hardly be seriously pressed, obviously recalls the bearer of the snaky locks and the deadly glances. Praxinoa emerges as a more colourful character than her friend and is certainly the more domineering. For all her affectation of carelessness (ll. 37–38) she outshines Gorgo in dress—a matter to which both, of course, pay a good deal of attention. Her chagrin when her fine attire is in danger from the crowd is of a piece with her volatile character. She is impatient, easily frightened, and capable of a deep emotion (ll. 82ff.).

Besides dress, the two love gossip and 'sights'. They regard their husbands as inferior-witted tyrants to be humoured—despite Gorgo's pretended plea for respectful mention of the father in front of his child. The child himself is treated with easy callousness by his mother, in her desire to be rid of him and off for an hour's distraction. Males encountered receive hyperbolic gratitude when they are useful, or a scornful tongue-lashing when they show disrespect. Women, conversely, are lauded as a sisterhood endowed with superior gifts (l. 146). However, Praxinoa's comment on the old woman at the palace gates conveys just that ambivalence in self-estimation which is the mark of this world's underdogs. The familiar lineaments of Theocritus' sketch may hold a particular fascination for us who live along the lines of a page of history on which a brave attempt to minimize the social disabilities of women is being recorded, with (since greed is still our problem) concomitant varieties of exploitation. However, we should notice that Theocritus does not condemn either the women or the society. He enjoys them and he offers them for our enjoyment, not our scorn, precisely as human beings and full of ludicrous failings. In this he is like Chaucer, and also like Chaucer views himself (witness Idyll VII) in no other light.

However, should any reader be preparing to fix eyes blinkered by current shibboleths upon this innocent sketch, he will find that it is not 'the woman question' that is to excite him to snorts of indignation, nor even, in all fairness, the Institution of Matrimony, but at best the inveterate domestic situation or battle of the sexes. The husbands are not on stage, but we have the impression that Theocritus knows them too, and that if they were, they would incur our merriment no less than do the Athenian husbands of Aristophanes' Lysistrata and her allies.

This poem's character as mime has already been mentioned (see General Introduction p. 16 and the introduction to Idyll XIV). The claim of one ancient commentator that the idea for Idyll XV was taken from a mime of Sophron about spectators at the Isthmian Games finds no corroboration, and it appears on the face of it that any dependence must be remote. A closer relationship seems to subsist with Herondas' fourth Mime, which concerns a visit to the temple of Asclepius at Cos and includes a description of the works of art seen there. Descriptions of the sort are, however, traditional in Greek poetry from that of the shield of Achilles onward, and they appealed particularly to the

Hellenistic taste for visual and decorative detail, such as is strikingly exemplified in the cup passage of Idyll I. The present poem, after its eighty lines of well-contrived dialogue, breaks suddenly into Theocritean lyricism when the figure of Adonis on the tapestry is described. The fact that this high feeling is expressed by the truculent Praxinoa serves as a measure of the impact of the beauty conveyed—though we may admit a certain sentimental hyperbole in her utterance of it, which partly accounts for the unsympathetic comment of the bystander. The fury he calls down upon himself reassures us that the woman so momentarily moved is the same Praxinoa who scolds her husband over the family shopping. Indeed the oath by Persephone —helpless bride of the stern lord of the Underworld—shows that once again she has the domestic 'master' in mind. Her concluding thrust (which in the original seems to refer proverbially to levelling off an empty measure) has more the force of our being 'weighed in the balance and found wanting' than of the short commons meted out to slaves.*

The poetic strain is renewed and this time sustained with all the power of Theocritus' poignant grace in the concluding hymn. This seems designed to extol, behind the god Adonis, the 'immortal' Berenice, mother of Ptolemy and Arsinoë II (see General Introduction), and implies that the poem was produced soon after her deification by her children, Theocritus' patrons at the time. The date of this event is uncertain. Arsinoë became queen ca. 275 B.C. and died in 270 B.C., at about which time Theocritus must have retired from Alexandria. Presumably Idyll XV was written between these years and soon after Idyll XIV (see p. 127 above).

As regards dramatic time, the season is autumn, when Adonis, a vegetation god, is being prepared for his annual consignment to the Underworld, whence he will return with the following spring to the arms of Aphrodite. With her, the goddess of generation (see the introductions to Idylls I and II), was Berenice associated in cult, as mother of the ruling divinity and his con-

*See Gow *ad loc.*

sort, and as appropriate to her already legendary charm and womanly virtues (cf. Idyll XVII). The tableau of the dying god who will be solemnly buried on the following day has, then, some of the abiding features of a harvest-season festival in the offerings of fruits and other produce, but the element of thanksgiving, prominent in the Demeter festival of Idyll VII, is here subordinated to the enactment of the mystery of the fruit that falls to the ground and dies that life may be renewed. It was no doubt the awakening of the Greek awareness to the mystery not merely of the life cycle but of its spiritual analogue that made the Adonia so popular a festival through much of the Greco-Roman world.

The Adonia, as is the tendency with cults which draw attention to the mystery of life—since physical and social incapacity, when, at least, they are accepted, imply a corresponding freedom from the power struggle—appealed chiefly to women. In Theocritus' poem, the queen gives the display, and the hymn and the obsequies are performed by women. Moreover, this explains Praxinoa's 'female chauvinistic' remarks and should be borne in mind as the background to Theocritus' whole mise-en-scène. That men also attended the male god, both in such official roles as that of armed escort (ll. 6, 51) and as spectators, is equally clear from the poem. About contemporary with this Idyll is an interesting papyrus found in the Fayûm, in which are recorded household expenses for the days of the festival, among which occur such items as garlands, (holy) water, an admission fee, and a vast expenditure on nuts and figs.* The inclusion of sums for bath and barber—an excessive amount, which, it has been suggested, covers a special ritual shaving—indicates a man, and indeed, as we see in Idyll XV, the master of the house would most often do the purchasing himself, unless perhaps he was wealthy enough to have a trusted slave as steward. The accounts may, of course, be for a whole household, but in any event they would appear to include a male devotee.

*See Gow, pp. 262–64, describing *P. Petr.*, III, 142.

The Devotees of Adonis

(Praxinoa and Gorgo)

GORGO
Is Praxinoa at home?
            PRAXINOA Gorgo dear! At last! Come in!
A wonder you got here at all. Pull up a chair for her,
    Eunoa.
A cushion for it.
            GORGO Please don't trouble.
                        PRAXINOA Do sit down.

PRAXINOA Do sit down.

GORGO
O my poor nerves! I was lucky to reach you alive,
Praxinoa, what with the crowd, and what with the chariots
    and horses:
the town's crawling with men in hobnail shoes and capes,
and the road's endless: you live further away than ever.

PRAXINOA
That's that half-wit. He took this hutch—we won't call it a
    house—
at the ends of the earth, to prevent you and me being
    neighbours:
10   he meant it to spite me, the hateful beast—always the same.

GORGO
My dear, you mustn't speak of your husband Dinon so
in front of the boy. Don't you see how he's staring at you!
It's all right, Zopyrion, sweetie: she doesn't mean Daddums.

PRAXINOA
Well I'm blessed! The brat understands.
                        GORGO He's a nice
    man, Daddums.

PRAXINOA

That Daddums of his! Why, only the other day we told him
'Buy some soda, Daddy, and some red dye from the store.'
The godalmighty fathead brought back salt!

GORGO

Mine's the same: money runs through Diocleides' fingers.
He bought five fleeces yesterday—dogs' fleeces!
Hairs plucked from some old bag—every one filthy!   20
Seven drachmas a fleece—always some new headache!
Look here, put on your best dress and your cloak; we're going
to the palace of rich King Ptolemy, to see the Adonis show.
I hear the Queen's making a splash.

                    PRAXINOA Affluence is for the affluent!
              GORGO What sights, what tales of sights you'll have to tell
to those who haven't seen them! Come on, it's time we were going.

PRAXINOA

'For the idle, life's one long weekend'. Eunoa!
The wool! Leave it lying about again and I'll flay you.
These cats just love a cozy doze. Move, won't you!
Bring the water, quick! I need the water first,   30
and she brings soap! Well, give it me!—Vandal! not so much!
Now the water—Numbskull! Did I tell you to soak my dress?
That'll do. I'm washed—as much as God wills!
Now, where's the key of the big chest? Bring it here.

GORGO

Praxinoa, that heavy-pleated gown does suit you.
Do tell me what you paid the weaver for the cloth?

PRAXINOA
Don't remind me, Gorgo! More than two silver minas,
and then I put my whole soul into the making-up.

GORGO
You've created the 'look' for you: that at least you can say.

PRAXINOA (*to the maid*)
40   Bring me my cloak and hat. Take care how you put it on.
I'm not taking you, child. Bogey get you. Horsey bite.
All right, cry! I'm not going to have you lamed, that's all.
Let's get going. Phrygia, take the boy and play with him.
Call the dog in, and mind you bolt the outer door.

Ye gods, what a frightful crowd! However are we to get
    through?
They're just like ants, countless millions! Well, Ptolemy,
you've brought us many a blessing since your father went
    to heaven.
We don't get scoundrels creeping up on passersby to rob
    them,
Egyptian-style, the sort of trick those gallows birds like
    playing—
50   birds of a feather, devil's playboys, damn them all!
Gorgo, darling, what shall we do? The King's war-horses,
they're on us! Don't trample on me, please, good sir. He's
    rearing,
the big bay! What a brute! Out of the way, Eunoa,
madwoman! He's going to kill the man who's leading
    him.
Thank heaven I had the sense to leave the child at home!

GORGO
It's all right, Praxinoa: we're behind them; they've gone on
to their stations.
                    PRAXINOA I'm feeling better already.
    There are two things

terrify me, ever since I was a child: a horse
and a slimy snake! Hurry! The crowd's just pouring in.

GORGO
Have you come from the palace, Mother?
OLD WOMAN Surely I have, child.   60

GORGO
Then it's easy to get in?
OLD WOMAN The Greeks got into
  Troy by trying.
Everything's done by trying, my pretty darlings, 'tis sure.

GORGO
So—the wise woman uttered in riddles, and was gone!

PRAXINOA
Women are wise to everything. Down to how Zeus
  wedded Hera.

GORGO
Praxinoa, just look how they're packed round the palace
  gates.
PRAXINOA Good grief!
Gorgo, give me your hand. Eunoa, you hold Eutychis'.
Hold tight, or you'll get lost. We'll all go in together.
Eunoa, mind you stick to us. Oh no! That's torn it, Gorgo!
Torn my summer wrap in two! For God's sake, man,
as you hope to prosper, have a care for my cloak.   70

STRANGER
Can't promise, but I'll watch out for it.
GORGO What a crowd!
They're jostling like pigs.
STRANGER Cheer up, lady, we're in the clear!

PRAXINOA

And may you be in the clear for evermore, dear sir,
the way you've sheltered us. What a nice, considerate man!
Our Eunoa's getting squashed. Go on, push, you ninny!
    Bravo!
'Ladies inside!' as said the man who bolted the door on the
    bride.

GORGO

Praxinoa, come over here. Take a look at this embroidery.
How fine it is, and delicate. Robes for the god is right.

PRAXINOA

Goddess Athene, what weavers, that could work them!
80 And what artists, that could draw such accurate figures!
How realistically they seem to stand, and even dance,
as if alive, not woven. Isn't man a marvel!
Here's the god himself, lying on a silver couch!
How lovely that is! The first down flowering on his cheeks.
O thrice-beloved Adonis, loved even in Acheron!

2ND STRANGER

You stupid women, can't you stop your endless burblings
like pigeons! They get on my nerves with all those slurred
    vowels.

PRAXINOA

Well I'm blessed! Where's *he* from? What's it to you if we
    burble?
You give your orders where you own; you're ordering
    Syracusans.
90 And let me tell you, we're descended from Corinthians,
the same as Bellerophon, so we talk Peloponnesian,
and I suppose you will allow that Dorians may speak Doric.
Sweet Persephone, let's have no more masters but the one!
If we don't measure up to *your* standards, so much the
    worse for you!

GORGO
Hush, Praxinoa! Argeia's daughter's about to sing
the hymn to Adonis. She's a wonderfully talented *artiste*.
Last year she took the prize for the dirge, and you can bet
she'll give a fine performance. She's clearing her throat
  already.

SINGER
  Lover of Golgoi and Idalion and craggy Eryx,
  Queen Aphrodite, player with golden toys: 100
  see, in the twelfth month the soft-footed Hours,
  the tardiest of the gods, the dear-loved Hours—
  How all mortals yearn for their coming and their
      guerdon!—
  bring you Adonis from ever-flowing Acheron.
  You, Cypris, Dione's daughter, made immortal,
  so men tell, the mortal Berenice,
  dropping ambrosia into a woman's breast.
  So, to give you joy, O many-named,
  and many-faned, does Berenice's daughter,
  Arsinoë, fair as Helen, shower   110
  with all delights Adonis. At his side
  are fruits, as many as the trees that bear them;
  tender cresses, nursed in silver baskets,
  golden caskets full of Syrian myrrh,
  patties such as women bake by platefuls,
  from white barley-meal and every spice,
  kneading some with honey, some with oil.
  All things that fly or creep are with him there.
  Green arbours, hung with scented anise,
  are built for him: the young Loves light upon them   120
  like fledgling nightingales who flutter on a treetop,
  testing their waxing wings from branch to branch.
  O the ebony, the gold, the ivory eagles
  bearing his cup-boy off to Cronian Zeus!
  The pile of purple rugs, softer than sleep!
  Miletus shall declare, and the Samian shepherd:

'Lovely Adonis' couch is all our work'.
Cypris holds him: his rosy arms are round her;
eighteen or nineteen years of age the bridegroom:
130   his kisses prick not; the down on his lips is golden.
And now fare Cypris well; she has her man.

Ah, no sooner shall the dew at dawn have fallen
tomorrow, but in cortège forth we'll bear him
to where the waves disgorge upon the shore:
hair unpinned, robes let fall to the ankle,
breasts bared, we'll raise the shrill dirge.
O loved Adonis, hither and to Acheron
you steal alone of half-gods. Not Agamemnon,
not that hero rage bore down, great Ajax,
140   not the firstborn of Hecuba's twenty sons,
Hector, not Patroclus, and not Pyrrhus who
alone returned from Troy, nor yet before them
the Lapiths, nor Deucalion's sons, nor Pelops',
nor the Pelasgian lords of Argos, could not.
Be gracious, dear Adonis: till next year.
Adonis, our love waits on your return.

GORGO
Praxinoa, isn't she a wonder-woman! Marvellous,
how much she knows; perfectly marvellous how sweet
    she sings!
It's time to go home. Diocleides hasn't had his dinner.
150   The man's all acid; you daren't go near when he's hungry.
Fare you well, Adonis dear—and we, till you return.

❧Idyll XVI

Theocritus' unsuccessful appeal for patronage to Hiero II of Syracuse (see General Introduction p. 9) is a work of characteristic charm and worthy of those Graces whom it honours. The wistful candour of both its lighter and its more solemn passages contrasts not only with the more ponderous Idyll XVII but also with the court poems of Callimachus (see General Introduction p. 11), which for all their art remain monuments to the spirit of sycophancy.

The themes that Theocritus here illustrates with his own grace are all commonplaces in ancient literature: the penury of poets, the stinginess of patrons, the uses and corruptions of wealth, the immortality bestowed by *poiēsis*, the praises of the victor-hero-patron, the prediction of woe to his enemies and prosperity to his subjects. Theocritus deliberately invokes the memory of poets before him who enjoyed patronage: Simonides overtly, for it is he who is referred to at line 43, and on whose declaration 'what life is there without pleasure?' Theocritus rings changes at lines 23 and 104–5. So must Pindar's prayer for Syracuse in his fourteenth Olympian Ode have echoed in the minds of Greek readers of lines 80ff., and it is Pindar's epinician (or 'victory') poems which provide the formal background for this albeit less solemn Idyll, and which also abound in mention of both Muses and Graces. Moreover, although in lines 36ff. it is the Thessalian patrons of Simonides on whom Theocritus elaborates, Hiero could not fail to recall that both Simonides and Pindar had received favour from his namesake, Hiero I of Syracuse. That Theocritus does not say explicitly that this is a reason for the second Hiero to act in like manner towards himself may be explained as tact. Hiero, it appears, (see below) was not yet king of Syracuse, and the roundabout allusion might serve to flatter ambition while preserving discretion. By contrast, the rather gratuitous-seeming reference (l. 29) to the duty of hosts to speed their guests when they would be going, has been thought to refer to the tyrant Dionysius I of Syracuse,* who regarded his entourage as ipso facto less than free agents—an example Hiero is urged to shun. At the same time it no doubt gives notice that Theocritus is not prepared to barter his own freedom of movement.

Idyll XVI's importance in Theocritean chronology has been discussed in the General Introduction. Its general tone, as there observed, is apposite, since in contrast to that of Idyll XVII it strongly suggests the innocent expectation of the poet, soon to turn in disillusion to a more mendicant and conventional flattery. It intimates also the openness of the scene: a Syracuse where Hiero had but newly taken over from Pyrrhus on the latter's departure for Italy and Greece, where he met his death. The assumption of an early date in Hiero's supremacy, while he was still general and not yet king, is supported by the absence from the poem of any reference to the latter title, and, more remarkably, by the informal, even bantering tone, hardly appropriate to the wearer of a Hellenistic *diadema*, even given the difference in prestige and manners between the courts of Syracuse and Alexandria. True, Hiero is likened to Ajax and Achilles, and these were both 'kings', but the comparison is in respect of martial prowess and the immortality bestowed by a poet. In any case, Homeric kings are a proposition entirely different from Hellenistic princes (Hiero is more properly *tyrannos* than *basileus*), being more warlord than sacred majesty—a character brought to the European tradition of kingship across Alexander's east-west bridge and first bodied in his heirs and in their posthumous cult of him.

An early date for the poem, shortly after 275 B.C., the year of Pyrrhus' departure, and before 273 B.C., to which we have speculatively assigned Idyll XVII (see General Introduction), is further attested by the references to the Carthaginians (Phoenicians),

*See Gow, p. 311.

who are said to be trembling in anticipation of a power that will drive them from their Sicilian outposts. We know that on his rise to power Hiero was created 'General against the Carthaginians', and such a mandate would presumably envisage their expulsion from Sicily, where they had long established colonies such as Lilybaeum, as a preliminary to their prosecution home. This would explain the benedictions on Sicily that the poet foretells following their expulsion (ll. 86 ff.)—a happy theme for him as the would-be bestower of immortality on the ruler of a prosperous land. Hiero's best-known encounter with Carthage (or the only one of which we have sure information, since the details of his reign are largely obscure) was as ally of Rome in the First Punic War, but this assuredly is not referred to here. That episode followed on a period of alliance with Carthage and formed a not altogether glorious climax to the victorious career of the by now well-established monarch of Syracuse. Here the picture is altogether different, with Hiero's successes still in the future and to be prayed for.

To Hiero, then, Theocritus proposes to come, poor but for 'our Graces'. Traditionally, the Graces (in Greek *Charites*) were handmaids of the Olympian gods, often associated with the Muses and sometimes said, like them, to be daughters of Zeus. Their cult was maintained at Orchomenus in Thessaly, where it had been established by the king Eteocles who in one version of the myth is their father (l. 100). They figure in the fragments of Simonides and Bacchylides and in Pindar act as intermediaries between gods and men by the mouths of those they protect and inspire. In Theocritus' poem they are characteristically demythologized (cf. the introduction to Idyll 1) so that they become personifications of his poetic inspiration, or even (as Gow holds) of his separate poems.* Certainly this view fits the passage in which, with wry disrespect, he depicts their behaviour on being rebuffed (ll. 8ff.). Yet that they are not simply to be equated with 'my poems' appears in the concluding lines. They still are personifications of that grace (since the New Testament has

*Gow, p. 308.

theologized the word, we might prefer to use 'charm') which supervenes upon mortal events, and which may attain immortal stature by the creation (*poïesis*) of poets, which is in the gift of the Muses: 'for what, without the Graces, lovely remains to man?' But, says Theocritus, if patronage is refused, that attainment is cut off. Then the 'Graces' (of the patron) are, as it were, inhibited by the poet's penury: or, in his witty metaphor, confined by his empty coffer!

Nor should the commonest sense of the (unpersonified) word *charites*, the sense of 'thanks', be excluded from Theocritus' artifice. Though it is impossible to render it in the English translation, 'Who will receive our *thanks*?' is an undertone to line 6, as is 'What, without *requital* is lovely to man?' for lines 104–5, or 'May I ever dwell with *gratitude*' for line 105. If anyone feels this is straining things unduly, he should consider that lines 10–11 would bring to the minds of Theocritus' Greek readers an anecdote of Simonides (constantly, as we have seen, in the background of the poem) where the *charites* in the chest are quite simply 'thanks'. I translate the account of Stobaeus, cited in Gow: 'Simonides, when someone called on him to compose an encomium and said he would recompense him, but gave him no money, said, "I have two chests, one for thanks and one for money, and when I open them, I find that of the thanks bankrupt, so far as the supplying of my needs is concerned, and only the other good tender." '*

It is not without art that Theocritus seems to confound Graces with Muses. At the outset he distinguishes them, disclaiming to be a mouthpiece of the Muses, since they inspire themes of the gods, whereas he aspires only to hymn a mortal. This is the same modesty that appears in Idyll VII and wherever Theocritus adverts to himself spontaneously, unhampered by such considerations as motivate Idyll XVII. It is the light in which the poet chooses to appear and it can seem remarkably candid. In the apostrophe to the Graces of Eteocles he means to affirm the mortal birth of the Graces in contradistinction to the Muses:

*See Gow, p. 308.

indeed all manuscripts but two late ones read 'daughters', not 'Graces', though the reading appears inferior. It is apparently in line with his professed modesty that he goes on to rank himself as only one among many poets who might celebrate Hiero's deeds; yet to these others he attributes the inspiration of the 'daughters of Zeus', the Muses, whose help he had earlier disclaimed; moreover, it is certain that in the passage beginning with the trumpet call 'All fair fame comes to men from the Muses', it is the Muses Theocritus is claiming to serve. Some have found the transition here oddly abrupt, and certainly the passage amounts almost to a reprise or new start. The point, I think, lies in the immortality theme and in Theocritus' aptitude for piercing the mythological trappings of things. Having elaborated the claim that poetry conveys immortality (to the Greek mind, the distinguishing feature of godhead* and therefore particularly appropriate to the divinized wearer of a *diadema*), he moves from his initial distinction between Grace and Muse to an identification which makes bold dramatic use of the traditional tendency to interchange their roles. Immortality, he is implying, the affair of the Muses, is precisely dependent upon the gift of the Graces. Muse and Grace, finally, are assumed to one another, so that when the poem ends, as it began, with the Graces, they are by now '*our* Muses', the emphatic position of the Greek possessive adjective contrasting with its position in the phrase 'our Graces' (literally 'Graces our') near the opening of the poem.

*Theocritus must be taken to be emphasizing immortality in this world, for as K. J. Dover points out, the average Greek of his day would have believed, not in the shades in Hades (here an anachronism), but in the reward of the good after death. (*Select Poems*, edited with an introduction and commentary [London: Macmillan, 1971], p. 216).

The Graces

(To Hiero)

The daughters of Zeus and the poets have ever this selfsame
    care,
to sing the praises of the gods and the glorious deeds of
    men:
the gods fall to the Muses to sing, for themselves are
    goddesses;
but we who, behold, are mortal—of mortals be our song!
For of all men who dwell beneath the cloudy sky,
who will unbar his house and warmly welcome our Graces,
instead of sending them packing without any presents?—
    whereon,
feeling belittled, home they trudge on their bare feet,
and grumble at me, because they return thus
    empty-handed!

10   Then they retire into the depths of my empty coffer,
and sit in a huddle, waiting, head on chilly knees—
ever their retreat when a sortie fruitless proves!
So I ask, who is there who, in this age, will befriend a man
who speaks his praises out? I know not. Men no more
are eager to be known for noble deeds. The law
of profit rules them. Hand in pocket, each one spies
for a stray shilling to carry away—won't even stop
to rub the tarnish off for a tip, but is quick to remark,
'Blood is thicker than water, and I could do with a little
luck myself.' Or, 'The poet's reward must come from the
20   gods.'
Or, 'Who wants to hear another ? Homer's enough for us
    all!'
Or, 'The poet most to my taste is one I don't have to pay.'
Gentlemen, what do you gain by lining your coffers with
    gold?
Wealth's blessing lies not therein, to those who have minds,

but in spending on soul's ease somewhat, and something besides
on a poet; in doing good to your kin, yes, and many
another man; in making continual offerings to the gods,
welcoming the stranger, giving him cheer at your table,
and in speeding him on his way whenever he will be going.
But foremost and first in revering the sacred bards of the Muses,　　　　30
that one day, buried in Hades, you may hear fair praise of yourself,
not weep unwept by the cold Acheron, like some churl,
palms calloused by the mattock, who bemoans
his portion from his father's—penury. Many a serf
in Antiochus' palace and King Aleua's drew monthly rations.
The Scopadae owned many a calf—they were herded, lowing,
to the byres with their horned sheep; and over Crannon Plain
were pastured by the shepherds of the worshipful Creondae
a thousand sheep, all choice. But not in these their joy
when it came to pouring their sweet lives out on old man Charon's　　　　40
broad raft, and all unheeding these many treasures
they left, agelong to lie among the poor dead!
All unremembered they, but that the bard of Ceos,*
godlike embroidering lays on his harp of many strings,
set their names on the lips of men unborn, and even
the swift steeds who brought them crowns from the holy games
received their meed of praise. For who would have heard
of the Lycian chieftains? Who would have known of Priam's sons
with their long hair or Cycnus of the womanish skin,

*i.e., Simonides.

50   had not the poets echoed the battle cries of old?
     Nor had Odysseus, after he roamed to every land,
     ten long years, and last at Hades' shore
     arrived alive, after escaping the bloody cave
     of the Cyclops—not even he had won undying fame;
     the swineherd Eumaeus had been silenced, Philoetius died,
     still busy among his kine, and the great-hearted Laertes,
     had the lays of a man of Ionia not dowered them with
          renown!
     All fair fame comes to men from the Muses,
     and dead men's riches the living undo. But to give good
          counsel
     to a man corrupted by greed is like counting the waves on
60   the beach
     as wind and bleak sea roll them landward; or trying,
     in water however clear, to cleanse a brick of clay!
     Good luck to such a man! Beyond all reckoning be
     his silver, and may desire for ever more possess him!
     But I prefer honour and men's goodwill before
     many horses and mules. I seek of mortals one
     to whom I may come, not unwelcome, bringing my Muses;
     for the poet who sets out on his way without the daughters
     of Zeus the Counsellor is apt to find the going uneasy!
     Not yet has heaven wearied of bearing the months and
70   years:
     many times shall her steeds turn the wheel of the day!
     And he is yet to come who shall find in me the poet
     of deeds as great as ever frowning Ajax dared,
     or Achilles, on Simoïs' plain by Phrygian Ilus' tomb.
     Already now the Phoenicians who dwell on the outermost
          fringe
     of Libya, under the setting sun, are shuddering. Already
     the Syracusans are grasping their spears by the middle and
          weighing
     their wicker shields on their arms, and Hiero goes among
          them
     girding himself like to the heroes of old, a plume

of horsehair shadowing his helm. Zeus, glorious father,   80
and Lady Athene, and you, maiden, who with your mother
have made your own the mighty city of the famed
    Ephyrians
by the waters of Lysimeleia: may evil constraints send
our foes from the island and over the Sardinian Sea,
    announcing
the fate of loved ones to children and wives—a remnant of
    so many!
May the dwellers of old return to the townships, ravished
    quite
by hands of vandals, and till the fields to fruitfulness; may
    the grasslands
fatten sheep by the thousand, the plain be full of bleating.
May cattle in droves returning to their stall hasten the
    steps
of the late traveller; the fallows be tilled against the seed
    time   90
when the cicada chirps in the trees and keeps his watch
over the shepherds beneath him in the sun. May spiders
spin their webs lightly upon armour, and the cry
of war be heard no more, but poets bear the name
of Hiero high beyond the Scythian Sea to where
Semiramis bonded her walls with asphalt and made her a
    realm.
Of whom I am one, but many another the daughters of
    Zeus
favour—may it be our task to sing the praise
of Sicilian Arethusa, her people withal, and the warrior
Hiero! Goddesses, Graces of Eteocles, who love   100
Orchomenus, city of the Minyae, enemy once of Thebes:
when no man calls, here I would stay; but if they bid me,
I will arise, and with our Muses hie me to their homes.
But leave you behind I will not, for what without the
    Graces
lovely remains to man? With the Graces let me live!

꧁Idyll XVII

In Idyll XVII the wellsprings of Theocritus' imagination are congealed, it seems, by the awful eye of Ptolemy Philadelphus, to whose scrutiny the poem is offered. It is not necessarily, like Idyll XVI, an appeal for patronage, but if it is not that it is something even less promising, the first dutiful return of a patronized poet. Comparison with Idyll XVI is inevitable, since both poems are dedicated to monarchs in whose patronage Theocritus was interested, and since the poem to Ptolemy appears to have been written no long time after that to Hiero (see General Introduction). But it is a pedestrian piece, lacking its precursor's felicity of invention, and the perplexity Theocritus expresses as to how to begin (l. 9) is real enough—only it is caused, one surmises, less by the multitude of Ptolemy's virtues than by their banality. However, having elected, not very originally, to start with Ptolemy's ancestry, Theocritus proceeds duly and dully through the obvious themes: the deities who can be found associated with the Ptolemaic family tree, above all the sainted Berenice—who has the advantages of being a real woman known to his generation and having the closest, most undoubted blood tie to the subject, her son, and moreover of having been posthumously exalted by him for the adoration of his subjects; next, his birth in Cos, the island subsequently of his predilection and —by what must have been a rare coincidence of tastes—also the poet's; the prosperity of his realm; the extent of his empire; his wealth and the good use he makes of it—not omitting the paying of poets; his singular piety towards his parents; his 'godlike' and irreproachable wedding to his sister.

All that we have to admire is the skill with which the poet manoeuvres himself through this 'labour' of duty. There is nothing wanting in the technical accomplishment—though his perverse method of enumerating the cities ruled by Ptolemy (ll. 76–78), which in the Greek produces a truly Alexandrian feat of versification, may leave us gasping with irritation rather than admiration; the comparable passage in Idyll XIV (ll. 52–54) has at least a dramatic propriety lacking here. The poem seems to owe some of its matter to two hymns of Callimachus, in which also Ptolemy receives his meed of adulation; at least there are themes in both the Hymn to Zeus and the Hymn to Delos that also appear here. Strictly, we do not know which poet wrote first, but when Theocritus makes the personified isle of Cos cry out for joy at Ptolemy's birth and bids the newborn monarch honour her 'as much as Phoebus Apollo honours blue-circleted Delos', it seems so plain that he has in mind the passage where Callimachus has Delos perform the same feat over Apollo that one is tempted to wonder if Theocritus is angling for the thanks of the court laureate as well as his master's. More charitably, we may suppose Theocritus, newly arrived on the Alexandrian scene, to have been so genuinely impressed by the undoubted talents of one high in the pecking order of poets as to have essayed to emulate them, but finding the great pedant's style an uncomfortable constraint on his more genial temperament, not to have repeated the attempt. The very least we can infer from the coincidence is that this was the sort of thing Ptolemy liked.

Another curious coincidence, though probably less significant, attaches to the opening of Idyll XVII, in which the poet makes a conventional bow to Zeus, seated, as it were, in his royal box, in the very words with which Aratus performs the same gesture at the opening of his *Phaenomena*.* This makes way for the drawing of a distinction between the god and the mortal subject of the poem which is reminiscent of the opening of Idyll XVI, except that this passage lacks the superimposed unifying theme of Idyll XVI, the relation between Grace and Muse (see the introduction to Idyll XVI). Theocritus, moreover, appears nervous of ranking Ptolemy too precisely as even the best of men, and hastens on to connect him with 'heroes sprung of demigods'

---

*Noted by Gow, p. 327.

—a thought that will later furnish him with some of the 'material' he professes, in the image of the forest of Ida, to find overabundant (the Greek *hylē*, like the Latin *materies*, means both 'wood' and 'matter'). In fact, the genealogy of Ptolemy left somewhat to be desired for a claimant to royal descent, let alone divine. His grandfather, Lagus, one of Alexander's generals, was not of particularly exalted birth. Arsinoë, Lagus' wife, however, (so it was claimed) traced her descent from Heracles through his son Hyllus and, on the way, King Amyntas I of Macedon (late sixth–early fifth century B.C.). Alternatively, since she had been, before wedding Lagus, a mistress of Alexander's father, Philip of Macedon, an established Heraclid, there were those who would salvage the Ptolemaic pretensions by making Ptolemy Soter, the usurper of Egypt after Alexander's death, Philip's son and thus half-brother to Alexander. Theocritus gives no countenance to this empty rumour. Nor does he make use of the helpful fact that the mother of Hyllus was Deianeira, according to one legend a daughter of Dionysus. And yet the mention of the Dionysiac games at lines 99–100 goes with other evidence external to this poem to show that the Ptolemies made much of this putative forebear.* Perhaps Theocritus preferred to leave the in any case abandoned wife Deianeira out of court in order to focus attention on Heracles' celestial bride, Hebe, goddess of youth (l. 31). She was more appropriate distaff kin to a family distinguished by the deified Berenice (see the introduction to Idyll XV), and it is for the set piece in Berenice's honour that the mention of Hebe forms the touchpaper.

*See Gow, p. 343.

An Encomium

(To Ptolemy)

Zeus be our point of departure, and Zeus the goal, Muses,
of our song's faring forth, for chief is he of immortals.
But of men, now, let Ptolemy be sung of first and last,
and middle too, for by far the best of men is he.
The heroes who of old were sprung of demigods wrought
noble deeds, and met with minstrels skilled to sing them;
so I, who like them understand my art, would sing
Ptolemy's praise. The gods themselves set store by song.
And yet, a woodman coming to tree-clad Ida would be
perplexed, in all that plenty, where to begin his labour.   10
What shall I first set down? A thousand I could name,
gifts wherewith the gods have showered the best of kings.

Ptolemy, Lagus' son, by birth was one to bring
a mighty task to completion, once it took hold on his
    mind—
a plan such as another man could not have conceived.
Equal honour his father gave him with the immortals,
and fixed for him a golden throne in the house of Zeus.
Beside him sits Alexander, and bears him friendly mien—
god the Persians dread, with his gleaming diadem.
And over against them is set, hewn from unyielding rock,   20
the seat of Heracles, dealer of death to the centaur.
There he shares in the banquet with the other children of
    heaven,
joying with all his might in his sons' sons, that Zeus
has lifted age from their limbs, and lives sprung of his own
bear immortality. (Forbear of both was a mightly Heraclid,
so the lines of both trace back to Heracles their source.)
And when he has feasted his fill of fragrant nectar, and hies
to his beloved wife's abode, to the one he hands his bow
and the quiver that hangs beneath his arm, to the other his
    club

30   of studded iron; with these they bring Zeus' bearded son
      to white-ankled Hebe's heaven-scented bower.
      And renowned Berenice, of wise women the pearl,
      the apple of her parents' eyes—Dione's august daughter,
      she, the Lady of Cyprus, had thrust her taper fingers
      into that fragrant bosom; wherefore they say no woman
      ever pleased her husband as Ptolemy's wife: he loved,
      and even more beloved! A man in such case may well
      be moved by love to the bed of his loving wife, secure
      if he trust his whole estate to his children, they're trueborn.
      But a wife without affection has ever her thoughts on
40   another;
      children enough are born, but never resemble the father.
      Queen Aphrodite, goddess surpassing in beauty,
      this you made your care; for your sake was Berenice
      the Fair exempt from crossing Acheron, river of groans,
      for you snatched her away before she could come to the
          sombre ship
      and the grim ferryman of the dead, and bore her away to a
          temple,
      and gave her a share of your honour; and gently on mortal
          men
      she breathes the balm of loves, makes light the pain of their
          longing.
      Dark-browed Argeia, to the man of Calydon, Tydeus,
      you bore the manslaying Diomede; and, deep-bosomed
50   Thetis,
      to the son of Aeacus, Peleus, you bore the spearsman
          Achilles.
      So peerless Berenice bore you, Warlord Ptolemy,
      to Warlord Ptolemy! From your mother's arms the isle of
          Cos
      received you, a babe newborn, and there you first saw day;
      for there had Antigone's daughter, in the grip of her child-
          pains, called
      on Eileithyia, who looses the girdle, and she stood by
      with a goodly will, pouring ease down all her limbs.

Lovely grew the boy, like his father in looks, and Cos
cried out in triumph, clasping the child in tender arms:
'Blessed be you, boy, and honour me as much   60
as Phoebus Apollo honours blue-circleted Delos.
In one and the same honour embrace the hill of Triops
and grant an equal favour to the Dorian cities nearby.
The Lord Apollo too has equally loved Rhenaea.'
So the island spoke, and a mighty eagle, bird of omen,
screamed from the clouds above, thrice, for a sign from
  Zeus:
for the majesty of kings is the care of Zeus, son of Cronos,
and it happens, if one he loves at birth beyond all others,
from that hour he makes good fortune attend on him, and
  gives him
the lordship over many a land, and a deal of ocean.   70
Myriad are the mainlands, and countless tribes of men
have wheat that the rains of Zeus nurture to ripeness, but
  none
so much as the low-lying land of Egypt grows,
where the Nile's overspill breaks and waters the clod;
nor has any so many settlements of skilled husbandmen,
for thrice a hundred cities are founded in Egypt, and then
thrice a thousand and thrice ten thousand and three times
  nine
and two times three—and of all Lord Ptolemy is king!
And he carves for himself slices of Phoenicia, Arabia, Syria,
Libya, and the land of the black Ethiopians. His word is law   80
to all the Pamphylians, to the spearsmen of Cilicia, to the
  Lycians,
the warlike Carians, too, and the isles of the Cyclades—for
  his ships
are the best that sail the deep, and all the sea and the land
and the sounding rivers are ruled by Ptolemy. Many a
  horseman
and shieldsman flocks to his standard, armed in glistening
  bronze.

In substance he outweighs all other princes, such the wealth
that rolls into his palace from all sides, day by day.
And his people pursue their callings at ease; no enemy
    crosses
the teeming Nile afoot to raise a shout in their hamlets
nor drives his ship up the beach and dons the breastplate to
90   raid
the Egyptians' cattle—such a lord sits throned in their broad
    plains,
the gold-haired Ptolemy, who can wield the spear and
    whose care is set
to preserve his heritage, as a good king should, and add to it
    somewhat.
Nor in good sooth is the gold heaped up in idle piles
in that wealthy house, like the store of ever-toiling ants,
but a goodly portion the gods' illustrious fanes receive,
in constant firstfruits offered, and many a gift beside.
Much has he given to mighty kings, to cities much,
and much to trusty friends. Nor to the holy games
100   of Dionysus comes one who can tune his song clear,
but he carries away a guerdon answering to his gift;
and in their turn do the Muses' spokesmen Ptolemy praise
for his bounty—and what fairer fame can wealth bring a
    man
than to be named among men? This the Atreidae have still,
when those myriad treasures won when they sacked the
    halls of Priam
are buried in the dark whence there is no returning.

And Ptolemy, alone of those who have died, of those whose
    prints
the dust their feet have trod on moulds, still warm,
has built for mother dear and father incense-fragrant
110   shrines, and set their images in, with ivory and gold,
resplendent saviours for mankind, and many a fatty
    thighbone
of oxen burns he there on altars running red,

as month by month revolves—he and his worthy wife:
than whom no better woman clasps in his halls her husband,
loving him with all her heart as brother and as spouse.
In such wise consummated was that holy union of
    immortals,
the pair the mighty Rhea bore, Olympus' suzerains;
and Iris, virgin still, must first purify with myrrh
the hands that strew their one couch for Hera and for Zeus.

Lord Ptolemy, fare well! Your fame I will record   120
with names of other heroes; and think no empty word
to utter to posterity. For virtue's substance pray to Zeus!

❧Idyll XVIII

The occasion of this lovely wedding song is unknown. The oddly emphatic opening, it has been said, suggests that an original introduction is lost or else that the poem forms part of some interchange, as do the contents of Idylls XI and XIII and perhaps Idyll VI (see the introduction *ad loc.*). The reference to the consecration of the plane tree (ll. 45ff.) has been thought to place the poem in the Hellenistic genre of *aitiai* (or 'causes', i.e., explications of legends underlying particular cults), and the existence of a tree cult of Helen at Sparta is said to be deducible from remarks in other writers. Or again, since we know from Plutarch that Helen and Menelaus were held in honour in Egypt (especially at Memphis, where one account said Helen was detained on her flight with Paris and never reached Troy), the piece may be part of Theocritus' Alexandrian output, and in this case might have reference to a royal or otherwise notable wedding there. Since we do not know, we can let the poem stand on its intrinsic merits and approach it simply as inspired by that commonplace theme of human invention, the marriage of the ideal pair: the bride of unique beauty and virtue who is won, amid keen competition, by a man of birth and wealth and valour. Helen, indeed, here looks very like a poetic ideal of womanhood. Her surpassing beauty, an inseparable theme from the third book of the *Iliad* on, may be the decisive factor in the choice of her as subject, but to beauty are joined skills more usually associated with Penelope, the archetype of wifely fidelity, than with Helen the *femme fatale*. However, we may recall that more homely glimpse of Helen returned to Sparta and duty which the *Odyssey* provides on the visit there of Telemachus in quest of his father, and the theme of the bride's accomplishments is anyway a commonplace of the Greek marriage encomium.

[160]

We find again the typical Theocritean charm that resides in the sophisticated poetic treatment of a theme very simply and naturally apprehended. Despite her idealized role, Helen is here free of her legend and appears, albeit matchless in birth and beauty, as one among her freeborn Spartan peers. It is as though the poet said, 'Helen has become a legend, but I will show her to you as she must have been before trouble overtook her.' The novel conception which places her squarely in her Spartan background, amid a gang of athletic young girls, devotees of Artemis and Athene, would seem to indicate something of the mind of one who, while he appreciates a conventional domesticity for his friends (see Idyll XXVIII), seems himself to yearn after some more ideal love than was provided for in normal Greek marriages. There is no indication that Theocritus ever married; certainly, unlike his friend Nicias, he seems not to have settled down to domestic life.

The free upbringing of Spartan girls (and those of some few other Dorian communities) was notorious throughout Greece, particularly for its emphasis on daily athletics, which elsewhere was thought appropriate for boys only. Spartan girls were trained to be the wives and mothers of warriors seldom at home. Boys, still in their childhood, were removed to barrack life under male supervision until, it might be, having at length (aged thirty) reached man's estate and been permitted to marry and breed more of their kind, they fulfilled the time-honoured parting injunction of their wives and were carried home from the annual campaign on their shields, bearing the frontal death wound that was the boast of their caste. True, these forms were institutionalized by the lawgiver Lycurgus and seem designed primarily to enable a relative handful of Spartiates to keep control over a numerically vastly superior servile class of Helots. Theocritus reads the spirit, at least, of Lycurgus back into the legendary past.

Apart from communal exercises, girls were left under their mothers' tutelage to learn such arts as gave honour to the goddesses, the warrior and the huntress, whose stern and virginal cults nourished the Spartan soul, and were thus fitted to take charge, perhaps, of a homestead worked by a considerable body of slaves. Doting mothers they might well be, losing their sons so early, to such female children as they were permitted to raise —daughters, by reason of their dowries and lack of usefulness as spear fodder, being an expense Greek fathers tended to balk at, so that everywhere far more girl babies were exposed at birth than boys. The passing reference to the mother of Helen ignores the legend of Leda, who became a swan and hatched the eggs from which sprang Helen and her brothers Castor and Pollux, and some said Clytemnestra, too, wife and murderer of Menelaus' elder brother, Agamemnon, who led the Greek expedition to recover her sister from Troy. Nor is Helen's paternity from Zeus, though mentioned, made much of by Theocritus. His interest in Helen's parentage is here limited to the wrench of the parting of mother and child-bride—a touch of the sympathetic insight we constantly find him evincing towards women.

Greek (and Roman) marriage ceremonies consist in the transfer, with accompanying religious sanctions, of a marriageable girl from her parents' home and authority to those of the suitor who has presented himself, or been attracted by a sizeable dowry, to be her husband. She is attended with song and dance by a band of bridesmaids, her compeers whose turn is to come, while she is duly escorted to her new home and as far as the door of the bridal chamber where she is to await the bridegroom, similarly escorted; beyond that, by a matron of honour whose duties are more intimate. These rituals are accompanied by a strain of badinage less restrained than is permitted in our society, indicated by Theocritus in the opening lines of the song discreetly enough not to interfere with the idealizing tone of the whole, yet suggestive of the free manners of the Spartan girls. In one of Catullus' marriage hymns (poem 62), the chorus of girls affects to lament over virginity lost, while the bridegroom's supporters are more realistic. The other (poem 61) is also instructive to compare with Theocritus' epithalamium. Although permeated by a more formal and solemn tone, it shows many common features of ritual: the procession, the chorus, calling on the name of the marriage god, Hymen, and so forth; but the puritanism of a thoroughly urban society and of the Stoic creed has infiltrated, so that although they crack 'non diu remoratus es' ('not long hast thou lingered') and bid the couple 'ludite ut lubet' ('Play as you please'), a ponderousness that is almost coy hangs over their words, hardly reminiscent of the sexual passion of which the same poet could write so much more directly when marriage and the duty of procreation were not in question. We may notice, too, that the looked-for child is in Theocritus compared to the mother, but in the Roman poet the point is all in perpetuating the father's family name and identity, which requires a son. Theocritus appears uninterested in the sex of the child—unless, indeed, in forecasting that it will inherit Helen's beauty, he means to point to a daughter, and specifically Hermione.

In this poem, as elsewhere, advantage is taken of the potential for irony that hindsight provides—a feature which makes it seem unlikely that the poem was composed for a contemporary wedding. The prayers to the three deities of lines 51–55, with their formal name-repetitions, will, Theocritus' readers know, scarcely be fulfilled, and in general the tragedy of the Trojan War looms behind the beauty and gaiety of the occasion depicted.

Epithalamium for Helen

Now once in Sparta, at the house of gold-haired Menelaus,
maids with hyacinths budding in their hair
set up their dance before the painted bride-room:
twelve, the cream of the city, a splendid sample
of Spartan womanhood. For Atreus' younger son
Helen the Fair had wedded, and he shut her in.
Together they sang one theme, and tapped the time
with weaving feet. The house rang with their bride-song.

What, fallen asleep so early, bridegroom dear?
10   Your knees gave way beneath you, did they? Did you nod?
Or was it from too much wine you collapsed in your bed?
If your mind was set on sleeping, you should have slept
alone, and left the maid to play with the rest,
by her doting mother, so late on into the night.
There's tomorrow, you know, and tomorrow's morrow,
    next year. . . .
Year in, year out, the bride is yours, Menelaus!

Happy groom! Some good soul sneezed on your way
to Sparta, with other suitors, to give you your win!
Zeus for your father-in-law! Alone among heroes,
20   a daughter of Zeus you have ta'en to you under one mantle.
None such as she is treads Achaean soil,
and a wondrous child she'll bear if it favour its mother.
For here be we, a band four sixties strong,
maidens all of her age, and we race together
by Eurotas' streams, and anoint ourselves like men;
and of all, not one is flawless, compared to Helen!
For fair is the face that the rising Dawn displays
to Night, as winter onward brings bright spring;
so Helen shone on us, golden in our midst.

As a mighty crop grows to adorn the ploughland,   30
cypress a garden, Thessalian horse a chariot,
so rose-skinned Helen grew to adorn Lacedaemon.
None wound such goodly yarn as she from her basket,
nor wove a closer web than that she wove
on her cunning loom and cut from its long beams;
nor surely another knows to strike from her lyre
a song of Artemis and broad-breasted Athene,
as Helen, on whose lids sits every longing.

You, fair and queenly maid, are now a housewife;
but we shall early abroad and down to the Track,   40
and the flowering meads, to cut sweet-breathing garlands,
with many a thought, Helen, for you: like lambkins
wanting the teat of their dam. The first we'll be
to wind you a wreath of the lowly-growing lotus,
and hang it on a shady plane tree; first to take
the liquid oil from a silver flask and sprinkle
under the plane tree's shade; and letters we'll cut
in the bark, that the passerby may spell them out,
Doricly: 'Honour me, Helen's tree.'

Bride, farewell; and farewell, bridegroom   50
of a famous father's daughter. Leto grant you,
Leto, nurse of children, a fair offspring;
Cypris, goddess Cypris, an equal love match;
Zeus, son of Cronos, Zeus, unstinting wealth
to descend in turn from sire to noble sire!

Sleep, breathe each love's longing into other's
breast, and forget not to wake toward the dawn,
at what time we will come, when the first cock
stretches his plumed neck out and calls from roost:
Hymen, hymenaee, joy this bridal!   60

Idyll XXII

This poem recounts two separate combats: a boxing match and an armed duel. In each episode one of the Dioscuri (the name means 'Zeus' boys'; they were the twin sons of Zeus and Leda, brothers of Helen), Polydeuces (or Pollux, in the Latin form) and Castor respectively, takes on a single adversary and overcomes him. It therefore falls into two parts, which require to be treated separately, particularly as they are curiously uneven in tone and execution. Indeed *prima facie* they present the appearance of having been composed at different times and with different purposes and subsequently welded into a whole by the writing of prologue, transition, and epilogue. It may safely be asserted that if only the prologue and the Polydeuces episode had survived, our faith in the integrity of Theocritus' craftsmanship would be undiminished, even if not much enhanced. The prologue celebrates in particular the role of the Dioscuri as patrons of sailors and contains an impressive evocation of the sea in storm and sudden calm. In this it draws consciously on the Homeric Hymn to the Dioscuri and frames this central passage with a suitably formulaic opening and close.

It looks as though the first episode was composed by Theocritus for the same reason as Idyll XIII—as a demonstration of how much more effectively the epic material of Apollonius of Rhodes could be handled as epyllia—at least, we may add, by a craftsman as skilled as himself.* In the *Argonautica*, the boxing match between Polydeuces and Amycus, king of the Bebryces, follows immediately upon the Hylas episode and both are placed on the nearer, westward side of the Hellespont, whereas Theocritus places them beyond, the identity of the Bebryces being, it

*See the introduction to Idyll XIII and Gow, p. 382.

seems, a rather blurry matter even to Greeks of education (however, the geographer Strabo later appears to agree with Apollonius). Again, comparison shows an overall similarity in the matter but must award the palm to Theocritus for artistry of presentation. He gives characteristic scope to his pleasure in the natural setting by lingering alliteratively over the clear water springing from the rock, and the various life to which it gives rise (cf. the springs in Idylls VII and XIII)—only that the crude violence of the overlord of this pleasant place may burst with the greater shock upon our lulled sensibilities. Apollonius has no such magic up the sleeves of his professorial gown, nor does he know how to stage-manage the meeting of the chivalrous Polydeuces with this uncouth monster so as to bring the quarrel naturally and inevitably out of their characters and situation.

The ensuing account is highly graphic and the modern reader needs to remember that, high-impact audiovisual entertainment being unavailable, the Greek had only the written and recited word to satisfy his vicarious bloodlust—also that the ancient boxing match was a bloodier affair than those our society permits. Certainly the Greek seems to have liked his more occasional draughts hot and strong, and did not insist that the battering stop short of death. So his gloves were leather straps bound round the hands and attached over the arms, the purpose being to sharpen, not cushion blows; the thongs might even have a cutting edge, as is illustrated by the well-known statue of a boxer in the Terme Museum in Rome. The invention of these instruments was indeed ascribed to Amycus, who was a sort of legendary patron of boxing. In Apollonius' account he produces the pairs to be used and boasts of his skill in fashioning them. (In Theocritus, we note, he chooses to be known simply as 'Boxer', so identifying totally with his art.) Moreover, it seems from many illustrations on ancient vases, as well as from literary sources, that Greek boxers aimed at the head, a blow elsewhere being regarded as a miss, if not a foul. Thus Amycus' chest blows are—to adapt our parlance—'below the collar', and the following assertion that his size was reduced from sweating is saved from total ridiculousness in scientific minds if we take it as describing generally the visual effect of his flustered state and inability to stand up to his opponent.

After this interlude, so instantly recognizable as of the enduring chivalric tradition of knight-meets-monster, the Castor episode comes as a rude moral shock. Scant honour accrues to the brothers, whom it takes some textual ingenuity to redeem from the role of downright cheats and thugs, our sympathies tending naturally to the side of their victims. It appears that a portion of text is missing, in which presumably Castor made some answer to the indictment of Lynceus. And it is possible that other redeeming features of the legend would be familiar to Theocritus' contemporaries but not to us: indeed Theocritus is our only source for this version, in which the daughters of Leucippus, prior to their abduction by the Dioscuri, were betrothed to their mutual cousins, the sons of Aphareus. In one more usual version of the story, the Dioscuri steal the necessary cattle for their brides' dowries from Aphareus, but the girls are not already betrothed. Although it may be questioned whether the theft of brides would be considered in the Heroic age much more dishonourable than the theft of cattle, the basic unit of exchange, it would appear that Theocritus, if he gave his own twist to the legend, was for his age underscoring the discreditable role played by the Dioscuri. The incident appears sordid in contrast to the valour of Polydeuces in his exchanges of words and blows with the boorish Amycus. At best it illustrates—apart from the ruthless prowess of Castor—their aptitude for relentlessly pursuing their own will. As Lynceus observes, the pair are inexorable—like the gravestone with which Zeus, their father, seconding their efforts, closes the doom of their opponents. Theocritus extracts only one 'moral' from the two incidents: that the Dioscuri 'are conquerors, and sprung of a conquering line'. It may be that this barren effect is what he intended, the Euripidean lesson 'See what the gods are like', and (as we have frequently noticed Theocritus using mythological material to treat of psychological phenomena) his 'moral' would pass through the intermediate—

and equally Euripidean—form, 'See the forces that govern our destinies', to the totally humanized 'See man, at once the hero and the bully', in which case the twin sons of Zeus personify each a side of the whole man.

I offer this interpretation of Theocritus' intentions as a likely one in view of the use he makes of his art to display human psychology, but if one adopts it one has still to admit that the poem does not succeed. The whole lacks artistic congruity and unity of treatment, and it remains very plausible that on this pretext disparate material has been put together and, for whatever reason, insufficiently reworked. Whereas the prologue and the Polydeuces episode bear criticism as poems in their own right, the Castor episode and the epilogue betray other signs of careless composition. Thus Lynceus describes the Dioscuri as carrying unsheathed daggers, but it later appears they are armed in the regular manner, each with two spears and a shield in his hands and a sheathed sword at his side. And in the conclusion it is implied that the Dioscuri are featured in the *Iliad*—which in fact, in its only notice of them, in Book III, states that they are dead. It would be possible, I suggest, to suppose that the two lines (in the Greek) that refer directly to the *Iliad* (ll. 203–4 in this translation) are a later interpolation, in which case the reference would be, acceptably enough, to the Homeric Hymn to the Dioscuri. Indeed, it is tempting to regard the whole second half of the poem as at least influenced by the accidents of transmission or the 'improvements' of lesser men—but in itself the desire to hold that Theocritus, unlike his model, never 'nods' would seem an insufficient reason for doing so.

While it does not dispose of the problem raised by these anomalies, a recently published suggestion seems worthy of mention: perhaps the two episodes in the poem are intended to provide contrasting samples of Theocritus' own preferred idyllic (Polydeuces) and the traditional Homeric (Castor) manner of treatment of themes.* This view would make Idyll XXII a further

---

*Carroll Moulton, 'Theocritus and the Dioscuri', *Greek, Roman and Byzantine Studies* 14 (1973): 41–47.

contribution to the dispute about contemporary poetic integrity that is reflected in Idylls VII and XIII. The implication is that the Castor episode is designed to fail—though the failure is on the plane of *mores* rather than of form: that Theocritus is in effect saying, 'See how unconvincing, nay, disreputable, we become when we try to Homerize our epyllia.'

The Heavenly Twins

The two sons of Leda and Zeus, who bears the aegis,
Castor we hymn and Polydeuces, dangerous to provoke
in boxing once his palms are strapped with the oxhide
   thongs.
On two counts and a third we hymn Thestias' daughter's
male offspring, the brothers twain from Lacedaemon;
for patrons they are of men who travel the dry land;
and then of horses, panic-stricken in the bloody fray;
and last of ships which have run into contrary winds,
   o'erweening
transgressors of the constellations' signs, their rise and
   setting:
so the winds raise a mighty billow at prow or stern,   10
or where they have a mind, and dash it into the hold,
bursting asunder the bulwarks on either side; the mast
hangs, and with it the tackle, all jumbled and torn;
and out of the sky, just as night is upon them, bursts
a mighty storm of rain: the broad sea is in uproar,
buffeted by the blasts and the iron patter of hail.
And yet will you, from the very depths, draw up the ship
and the sailors too, who thought their last hour upon them;
and of a sudden the winds cease, and a shining calm
lights upon the deep; the clouds depart their ways;   20
the Bears shine out, and between the Asses is seen,
dimly, the Manger: all the signs are for fair sailing.
O saviours both of men, and men's friends both!
Horsemen both, and harpists, athletes, poets! Which
shall I begin with? Castor? Or first with Polydeuces?
My song shall be of both, and of Polydeuces first.

When *Argo*, then, had slipped between the Clashing Rocks
and the menacing jaws of snowy Pontus, she came to the
   land
of the Bebryces, bearing the gods' dear sons, and there
   disbarked

30   that multitude of men from Jason's ship, by the ladder
      at either side, and setting foot on the deep sand
      of a shore swept by the wind, they strewed them beds, and
          plied
      the fire-stick in their hands. And Castor, the swift
          horseman,
      and swart Polydeuces sought solitude together,
      and wandered away from their comrades to inspect the wild
          wood
      of every kind on the mountainside. Under a smooth rock
      they found a living spring, brimming sheer with water;
      the pebbles gleamed from its depths like crystal or silver;
          nearby
      grew lofty pines, poplars, planes, and the pointed crests
40   of cypresses, and as many scented flowers—work belov'd
      of the furry bees—as carpet the meadows when spring is
          ending.
      And there sat basking a man of prodigious size and aspect,
      his ears scarred over with welts that fists had raised,
      his chest rounded monstrously and his back a broad expanse
      of forged flesh—for all like an armour-plated colossus!
      The muscles stood out sharply at the head of his brawny
          arms
      like the rounded stones which a winter torrent rolls and
          grinds
      smooth in its powerful eddies, and across his back and neck
      a lion-skin hung down from the clasped ends of the paws.
      Polydeuces, that prize athlete, was the first to speak, saying,
50   'Friend,
      joy to you, whoever you be! What men inhabit these parts?'

AMYCUS
What joy can I have, to see men I never yet set eyes on?

POLYDEUCES
Courage! They warrant you see just men and just men's
    sons.

AMYCUS
Courage I have. Is it likely that you should teach me that?

POLYDEUCES
Are you a savage—always spiteful and overbearing?

AMYCUS
I am such as you see me—at least no trespasser in your land!

POLYDEUCES
Would you might come there! You should return home, and
    with gifts.

AMYCUS
First, I'll none of your gifts, and second, I've none to spare
    you!

POLYDEUCES
As a gentleman, would you not give us some of this water
    to drink?

AMYCUS
That you'll know when thirst is parching your lips to
    faintness.   60

POLYDEUCES
Is it silver you need to persuade you? Or what is your price?
    Will you name it?

AMYCUS
Stand up, then, and raise your hands in single fight!

POLYDEUCES
At boxing? Or do you mean an all-in wrestling match?

AMYCUS
Landing out with your fists—you'll have need of all your
    skill.

POLYDEUCES
With whom, then, are my thonged hands to come to blows?

AMYCUS
You see him by you—no wenchling! You can call him
   Boxer.

POLYDEUCES
And is there a prize at hand, for which we are both to fight?

AMYCUS
Your slave am I, and you are mine, if I shall win.

POLYDEUCES
This is more like the strutting of crimson-crested cocks!

AMYCUS
70   Whether like cocks or lions, we'll fight for no other prize.

So Amycus took a shell and blew a hollow blast.
The sound died, and the Bebryces, whose hair is never cut,
speedily gathered under the shade of the plane trees, while
   Castor,
the Mighty in Battle, likewise went to summon, to a man,
the heroes from the Magnesian ship. Amycus and
   Polydeuces
armed their hands with the oxhide thongs, and the long
   straps
they wound around their arms, then stepped to the
   encounter
snorting murderously! And there began their hour of trial,
as long they contested which should take the sun on his
   back.
80   And in skill did you outrun the big man, Polydeuces:
the rays of the setting sun beat full into Amycus' face,
and wroth in soul he set on, aiming blows with his fists.

But the son of Tyndareus caught him as he came, on the
   point of the chin,
and he lost his former swagger, beginning to lash out wildly
and pressing forward furiously, his head bowed down to
   the ground.
The Bebryces cheered him on and from the other side
the heroes were putting heart into mighty Polydeuces.
They feared, in that narrow space, the Tityus-like creature
might get him down and vanquish him. But the wily son of
   Zeus
cut him on either side, with a right and a left in turn,   90
and stopped Poseidon's son in his tracks, huge though he
   was!
And there he stood, punch-drunk, and spitting out crimson
   blood;
and the Greek chiefs cheered to a man, as they saw the
   grievous weals
round mouth and jaws, and the swollen face, and the eyes
   like slits.
Then Lord Polydeuces baffled him, feinting blows on all
   sides,
and seeing him off his guard, smashed with his fist on the
   forehead,
in the middle, over the nose, stripping his brow to the bone.
So struck, he measured his length, on his back in the carpet
   of flowers,
but was up again, and grim the struggle resumed, as they
   tried
to batter each other to death with the rigid thongs. But the
   chief   100
of the Bebryces delivered his blows on the chest, well clear
   of the neck,
whereas dauntless Polydeuces pounded with ugly blows,
full in the other's face, and the flesh of Amycus fell,
from sweating, so that he dwindled in size. But Polydeuces'
   limbs

gained greater strength with labour, and an ever more
    vigorous hue.
But how did the son of Zeus bring down the monstrous
    man?
Tell, goddess, for you know, and I am only a spokesman
to voice what matter you will, in whatever manner you
    please.
Then know that Amycus, anxious to gain some signal
    advantage,
110   grasped with his left his opponent's left, and leaning aside,
and away from his guard, swung in on the other an upward
    right
from the flank—and had injured the Amycleans' king, had
    he
not turned aside his head and landed out with his fist
below the left temple, putting his shoulder into the blow.
The dark blood started, and poured from the gaping temple.
Then he struck him a left to the mouth, so the clenched teeth
    rattled;
and the blows rained thick and fast, till his face was
    disfigured,
the cheeks caved in, and headlong he fell to the earth,
dazed, and raised both arms to beg him 'Hold, enough!'
120   He was close to death, but, Boxer Polydeuces, you,
though victor, wrought him no doom; but he swore you a
    great oath,
calling upon his father, out of the sea, Poseidon,
to witness he never would wilfully molest a stranger again.

So, prince, of you I have sung, and, Castor, now of you,
Tyndareus' son, the horseman, the warrior clad in bronze.

The two sons of Zeus, having seized a pair of maidens,
the daughters of Leucippus, were bearing them off. But
    there followed
two brothers in hot pursuit, the sons of Aphareus,
Lynceus and mighty Idas, to whom they had been betrothed.

And when they arrived at the tomb of the dead Aphareus, all 130
leapt to the encounter, with one accord, from their chariots,
laden as they were with spears and hollow shields.
And Lynceus spoke thus, shouting from under his helmet,
'Sirs, out to make trouble, are you? What do you mean by this
brawling for other men's brides, with naked blades in your hands?
To us it was Leucippus betrothed these daughters of his;
long before you appeared, he gave us his oath we should wed them.
But you, to your shame, had designs on other men's brides,
and changed his mind, with your mules and oxen and other possessions,
filching a marriage for bribes! And I, a man of few words, 140
have often enough addressed you both to your faces thus:
"My friends, you act in a way unworthy of chivalry
when you woo to wife women whose husbands have been provided.
You have all of Sparta, all the horse country of Elis,
Arcadia's sheep pastures, and the citadels of Achaea,
Messene, Argos and the whole Corinthian coastline is yours,
where thousands of girls are reared by their parents, with no defect
of beauty or sense, and an easy thing it were for you
to marry wherever you pleased, for many a man would be willing
to take to himself a noble lord for his son-in-law. 150
And you are the flower of nobility, you and your fathers before you,
and all your ancestral line. Then, friends, allow our marriage
to come to fulfillment. We all will seek another for you."
All these things I said, but they fell on the empty wind,
and were blown to the sea-waves. No profit attended my speech.

For you two are inexorable and unbending. Yet, even now,
let us persuade you. You both are our father's brother's
     sons.'

CASTOR

· ·
But if you've a stomach for battling, and bathe we must our
     spears
in kinsmen's blood by unleashing this brawl, let Idas and
     my brother,
160 strong Polydeuces, refrain their hands, keep clear
of the fight, while we, the two younger born, I and
     Lynceus,
resolve the issue by Ares' might. Let us not bequeath
a great grief to our parents; one death is enough, in one
     house.
Let the others, intact, gladden their friends with bridals,
not funerals: let them marry those maids; it were fitting
at the cost of a little ill, to avoid a long vendetta.

He spoke, nor did the god bring his words to nought.
For the two who were older took the armour from their
     shoulders
and laid it down, and Lynceus advanced into the midst,
170 swinging his trusty spear to and fro, its tip
under the outer rim of his shield. And Castor likewise
brandished his spearheads; on both their crests the plumes
     nodded.
And first they were hard put to it, aiming at one another
wherever they might espy a glimpse of flesh exposed.
But before any hurt was inflicted, the spears had stuck fast
in the formidable shields, and shattered; and drawing both
their swords from the scabbard, again they wrought each
     other's bane,
with never a break in the fighting. Many a blow sent Castor
home on the broad shield, and the helm with its horsehair
     plume,

and many the sharp-eyed Lynceus landed on Castor's shield,   180
and even up to the crimson crest advanced his blade.
He was aiming a sharp thrust at the left knee, when Castor
stepped back and chopped the top of his sword hand.
   Stricken,
he dropped the weapon and started to flee to his father's
   tomb,
where stout Idas was lying, watching his kinsmen fight.
But the son of Tyndareus darted after, and drove his blade
clean through flank and navel, and straight the bronze parted
the bowels within, and Lynceus tottered and fell on his face,
and the heavy sleep of death sped down to close his eyes.
Nor yet was Laocoösa to see her other son   190
joined in happy wedlock at his father's hearth, for he,
Messenian Idas, quickly tore up the stone reared
upon Aphareus' tomb, to smite his brother's slayer.
But Zeus saved him, striking with one flaming bolt
the graven marble from his hands, and Idas to ashes.

And so it is no light matter to cross Tyndareus' sons,
who are conquerors themselves, and sprung of a
   conquering line.
Farewell, children of Leda: send good fame to attend
my songs, for all poets are dear to the sons of Tyndareus,
and to Helen, and all the heroes who aided Menelaus   200
in sacking Troy. The bard of Chios has wrought you glory,
my lords, in singing of Priam's city, the Greek ships,
the battles about Ilium, and Achilles, the pillar of war.
And I in my turn bring you these dainties from the Muses'
clear tongues, such as themselves provide, and such
as my house affords, for songs are the gods' finest tribute.

❧Idyll XXIV

Idyll XXIV retells an ancient legend in Theocritus' own manner, only here his motive is not to be explained, as was the case with Idylls XIII and XXII, in terms of contemporary literary controversy. It should be noted at the outset that one papyrus gives the scanty remains of the otherwise missing thirty-odd concluding lines, of which fragments the most coherent is a marginal note indicating that the poem ended in an appeal to Heracles for victory. Thus it appears to have been composed for a competition —information that needs to be borne in mind, as it can be expected to be material to the work's interpretation.

We have found Theocritus drawing on Pindar before, and it is not surprising that Pindar's fifth-century retelling of the ancient legend of the snakes sent by Hera to devour the infant Heracles should lie in the background of Theocritus' version of the same tale. Indeed, no literate Greek could have been unfamiliar with the first Nemean Ode, where the story is used in illustration of the virtues of Chromius, the charioteer for whose victory in the Nemean Games the ode was composed. 'Strength', observes Pindar, in a characteristically gnomic maxim, 'acts in deeds, and intelligence in counsel.' He proceeds to associate this latter virtue particularly with the power to foretell the future, represented in his poem by Tiresias, whose extreme age and weakness form an implicit contrast to the extreme youth and prodigious strength of Heracles; for though Pindar makes no mention of Tiresias' age, nor of his blindness, both features are as inseparable from his legendary persona as his mantic powers.

Theocritus seizes the opportunity to elaborate a striking picture out of the Tiresias episode, but seems uninterested in Pindar's maxim. Yet he has not been insensitive to Pindar's latent paradox of the wisdom of age and the strength of youth—a

commonplace in Homer and subsequent Greek literature—
which his poem seems to illustrate by design. It is Pindaric to
be sententious, and Theocritean to be graphic, and so we find
Theocritus lingering likewise over the evil aspect of the snakes
and imagining for us Amphitryon's actions when roused by his
wife's alarm. (Pindar chooses this dramatic moment for some
rather gratuitous moralizing about how differently men react to
their own troubles and to those of others.) But the most striking
difference is the domestic interest with which Theocritus has
invested what is for Pindar a heroic tale.

To begin with, the house does not resemble the heroic palace
in which Pindar leaves us to imagine Amphitryon at mess with
his warrior peers while his wife gives birth in the women's
quarters. Its layout has been a rather vexed question, but the
best explanation the present writer can concoct is that it consists
of a central hall approached from the house doors (probably
through a vestibule) with a number of (doorless) recesses open-
ing off it, one of which is the bedchamber of Amphitryon and
Alcmene, and another occupied by the babies. This would ac-
count for Alcmene's being able to hear but not see them, for it is
not likely that unweaned children would be shut away from
their mother. This arrangement is at the same time the likeliest
inference from the miraculous light which seems to flood the
whole house—or rather the main portion of it where the family
sleeps, for the servants are not roused by it and it seems that the
doors referred to by Amphitryon shut off their quarters from
the family dwelling and are barred on the inside. The servant
who sleeps by the millstones that it is her job to turn is of an
inferior order, as is also suggested by her rather quaint and pithy
style of speech. She serves conveniently as an intermediary to
convey Amphitryon's order to the servants' wing, since the
heavy dividing doors have cut off the sounds of his voice and of
Iphicles' shrieking. We may therefore suppose her lodged in a
courtyard or outhouse adjoining the main hall and servants'
wing.

The above seems a reasonable reconstruction from the data
given, though we have to admit that Theocritus, as is like him,

has not been at pains to make his mise-en-scène clear. However, we may suppose that the house he had in mind, albeit rather vaguely conceived, was of a style more familiar to him than an epic palace. Indeed in this peaceful domestic setting only the shield in which the babies are laid and the scabbard of Amphitryon remind us of his heroic status, so that the latter part of the poem, in which his chariots and his prowess in driving them are Homerically recalled, comes as an odd contrast, and we have the impression that Theocritus has lost interest and is merely filling a bill. It is the realization of the domestic scene that grips him: the maternal tenderness of Alcmene which strikingly opens the poem, the interaction of her alarm and the trusty response of her husband, the baby's innocent amusement at his prize, and gesture towards his father. In Pindar, Heracles' feat is seen through the eyes of Amphitryon, and it is at least natural that a newborn baby should not express any consciousness of achievement! We may note too that in jettisoning Pindar's timing of the snakes' onslaught, immediately after the birth of twins, Theocritus has turned the exploit in the direction of naturalism, since a ten-month-old baby could at least grasp a snake, whereas a newborn one could not even raise its head, as the Pindaric Heracles is made to do.

The direction of Theocritus' shift from Pindar is apparent, too, in his staging the incident by night. His Hera is taking no chances on either the mother with her women or the father with his peers intervening in time to save the child. This is a gain in verisimilitude. Moreover, it makes way for all the maternal and domestic touches that delight the poet and prepares for the dramatic shock when the peaceful household awakes to fear and alarm. The night setting makes way, too, for replacing the armed warriors, who in Pindar rush to bring succour, with the servants of the house, who are needed to bring light, and thus advances the poem's trend from the heroic to the domestic. Theocritus is at pains to avoid the tale's heroic antecedents, even to the omission of all mention of the city of Thebes or of any definite locality for the drama. It will be shown that the probable reason for this is bound up with the occasion of the poem's composition.

As for Alcmene, she dominates Theocritus' poem or at least the better part of it, and is to be classed among the Theocritean 'heroines', who include Simaetha, Cynisca, Praxinoa, and Helen. We may perhaps regret that, whereas in Pindar the just-delivered mother springs naked from the bed to combat the snakes, in Theocritus her action is restricted to waking her husband when herself alarmed by the strange light and Iphicles' cries. However, Theocritus' Alcmene is by no means deficient in character and nobility, nor in action where appropriate to her role as mother and queen, as when she initiates the interview with Tiresias. It may appear to modern consciousnesses that Theocritus' deepened appreciation of maternal love and conjugal closeness has entailed a less dramatic role for the woman, yet it is Alcmene and not Amphitryon or even Heracles who is the central figure for the greater part of the poem. Once again, Theocritus lovingly displays the human dignity of a realistic woman without denying her feminine role and therefore character. In this he has no doubt learned from Homer, and much from Euripides, but his native interest and insight are what differentiate his drawing from the wooden background figure who performs her set heroic action when Pindar pulls on the appropriate string, then to relapse into insignificance.

Even though it is as mother of her son that Alcmene will have undying fame, the superficial conclusion that therefore the fame will be undeserved would hardly occur to Theocritus, any more than to Homer. Indeed, it is in keeping with the emphasis of the legend that Amphitryon appears in a secondary role as educator, while it is from Alcmene that Heracles derives his heroic inheritance and, as it were, substance. And this despite the fact that there is no necessary suggestion in Theocritus' poem that Heracles is Zeus' son and not Amphitryon's (the words I have rendered 'known as the son of Amphitryon' can easily imply not a false supposition but a claim to distinction). The received legend tended to ambivalence on this point, one version running that the twins were of different fathers—the situation which Plautus was later to exploit for its comic potential—and thus supplying a ready motive for Hera's hatred. Pindar had already dealt with this account, for when he has Amphitryon rejoice in his son's marvellous strength, he is careful to tell us that the gods had 'set down as a retractation for him' the other account. If, as seems possible, Pindar is, by this careful phrasing, still leaving the gods' veracity in question, it would be like Theocritus to seize on the implication that the 'gods' were answerable to nothing more than the actual state of Amphitryon's mind and to advance the myth's stage of exposure towards rationalization (that is, explanation in purely human terms). This state of consciousness would account for any residue of ambivalence in the word 'known' alluded to above.

Clearly in Theocritus' version Zeus (one is, as often with Theocritus, tempted to write 'Zeus') has some particular interest in protecting Heracles, while Hera has some particular grudge against him, neither of which would seem sufficiently accounted for by the prediction of his future prowess and final apotheosis and union (in a Jungian sacred marriage) with their joint offspring, Hebe (Youth). And the miraculous strength and courage of the infant needs some supernatural explanation. Still, in Theocritus, divine intervention is well on the way to becoming marginal and inessential, and when subtracted, leaves us with a quasi-Nietzschian Heracles setting his infant foot on the first rung of an ascent, via the progressive conquest of the evil forces of this world, to that consummation of human potential which is conceived as divinization. However, we should be cautious. Theocritus' values are not Nietzsche's, and his Greek superman is at the same time a remarkably engaging figure. His baby glee in his trophies, his admirably conventional deportment as boy and youth—even his traditional capacity for food becomes the virtue of temperance, since he exercises it only once a day—we owe to the genial temperament of his maker, which is also to say to the poet's age and circumstances. For Heracles emerges very much as a Hellenistic ideal gentleman, complete with all proper accomplishments; indeed it is this blueprint which overshadows the boyhood section of the poem, repressing the spontaneous charm of the Alcmene episodes.

This aspect of the poem chimes in with the historical fact that the house of Ptolemy boasted of its descent from Heracles (cf. the introduction to Idyll xvii), to suggest that we are back in Theocritus' Alexandrian period, and that the competition for which these verses were written took place at a public festival in honour of Heracles. It is in addition feasible that in celebrating his ancestor, Theocritus is intending an identification with Ptolemy Philadelphus himself. If this were the case, it might also furnish the motive for the care with which Theocritus has described the night sky at the outset of his poem. It seems that the Bear (Ursa Major) is at its zenith, and is about to follow the path of Orion over the (western) horizon, where the hunter's shoulder (the star Betelgeuse) shows awhile after the rest of the constellation has set. It is some hours short of midnight, at which time, it is stated, the Bear itself will set; and it is dark. This datum of evening darkness, together with the mention of the babies' woollen blanket, points to the winter, and the position of the stars more accurately to February.* Since Heracles is stated to be ten months old, this would place his birth in April, the month of Ptolemy's birth and ascent to the throne. In any case, the identification would be bound to spring to the minds of Alexandrian courtiers, to whom nothing could seem more natural than that a patronized poet should glorify his patron under all possible guises. If, from egalitarian predilections, we are prone to condemn Theocritus for lapsing in the second half of this poem into the servility we have deplored in Idyll xvii, we have at least the moral consolation of observing that here, as there, it has debilitated his muse.

*This season was determined by astronomical calculations made by Eddington for Gow, p. 417, from whose understanding, however, I differ somewhat, as he, mistakenly it seems, regards midnight as the hour of Hera's onslaught.

Baby Heracles

When Heracles was ten months old, it happened one time
that his mother bathed him—Alcmene, princess of
  Midea—
with his brother Iphicles (who was younger by a night)
and filled them up with milk, and placed them both
in the bronze shield which had been Amphitryon's prize
when Pterelaus fell—and a fine piece it was!
And now, a hand on each of their heads, she said,
'Sleep, my babes, sleep sweetly till you wake;
sleep, little brothers, my joy, my blessed children;
10 peacefully slumber, peacefully through to daybreak.'
So saying, she rocked the great shield till they slept.
At the time when the Bear turns to his midnight setting,
over Orion, who shows his mighty shoulder,
then wily Hera set on two dreadful monsters,
snakes awrithe with glossy blue black coils,
by the threshold stone where the doors stand in their
  grooves.
Onward the two things rolled, uncoiling on the ground
bellies thirsty for blood, and darting from their eyes
an evil spark as they came, and spitting out venom.
20 But as with flickering tongues they approached Alcmene's
beloved children, they on the moment awoke,
for Zeus knew all, and the house was bathed in light.
And Iphicles, catching sight of the ugly beasts
with their wicked teeth, over the rim of the shield,
screamed outright and kicked off the woollen blanket,
struggling to escape. But Heracles leaned forward
and grasped them both in a vice of iron, by the throat,
where lies the deadly venom in snakes accursed,
which even the gods abhor. Yet again and again
30 they threw their coils around the boy late born,
milk-fed from birth, and tearless ever; again
relaxed their spines, striving in their distress

to find release from his unrelenting grip.
Alcmene heard the cries and roused her first:
'Rise up, Amphitryon; a horror has me in its clutch!
Up! Stay not to tie your sandals on.
Hear you the boys—the younger, how he howls!
Do you not know, it is dead of night—and the walls
are all lit up, as though with morning-shine!
There is something strange in the house, believe me,
     husband!'   40
She spoke, and he heeded his wife and left the bed,
going straight for the ornate sword which was ever slung
from a peg above the cedar couch. He reached
for the new-woven sword-belt, supporting the scabbard,
a heavy work of lotus, with the other hand.
And again the spacious chamber was filled with darkness.
Then he cried to the house slaves, in their stertorous sleep,
'Quick as you can, bring fire from the hearth, my servants!
Unbar the massy bolts of your doors!' And a woman,
a Phoenician, whose bed was by the millstones, shouted,   50
'Rouse you, patient carls; the master calls!'
Swift they appeared, hastily lighting their lamps;
the house was filled with hurrying feet—and then,
straight as they beheld the infant Heracles
grasping the creatures twain in tender palms,
so resolute, they gasped in horror. He held out the reptiles
to his father, Amphitryon, dangling them aloft
in baby glee, and laughing laid at his feet
the two terrible monsters, stricken by death.
Then Alcmene took to her bosom Iphicles, parched   60
and beside himself with fear, and the other boy
Amphitryon placed under the fleecy blanket;
then bedward turned, bethinking him of sleep.

In early morning, at third cockcrow, Alcmene
sent for Tiresias, seer of every truth,
and related the strange event, and urged him tell her
what should come of it. 'Let no false respect

for me conceal if the gods mean mischief. Truly
whatsoever the line the Fate hands down
70 from her distaff, it is not given to man to escape.
Son of Eueres, I teach you what well you know!'
So spoke the queen, and he answered her, 'Take courage,
lady noble-born, of Perseus' blood!
Take courage; have better hope of things to come.
Yea, by the dear light that long has left
my eyes, many shall be the Achaean women
who sing Alcmene's name as their hands roll
the pliant yarn around their knee at twilight.
A marvel shall you be to the women of Argos.
80 For this your son shall mount to the star-laden
heaven—so ample-hearted a hero he,
excelling other men and every beast.
Destined is he to make his home with Zeus
after he has accomplished labours twelve.
A Trachinian pyre shall have his mortal part,
and he shall be by marriage son to the gods
who sent those lurking serpents to devour his childhood.
Indeed that day shall dawn when the ravening wolf
shall lack all lust to pillage the kid where he lies!
90 But, lady, have ready fire beneath the ashes
and a pile of dry kindling—thorns or brambles,
or the wild pear all twisted by the wind.
Then burn these two snakes on wildwood faggots,
at dead of night, when they sought to devour your child.
At dawn, have one of your handmaids gather the ashes
and carry all with care across the river,
beyond the bounds, and throw on the jagged rocks,
and so return without a backward glance.
But first the house must be purged with flower of sulphur,
100 then pure water mixed with salt be sprinkled,
as is prescribed, with a wool-wound frond,
and an offering made, a hog, to the Upper Zeus:
so may you have ever the upper hand of your foes!'

Thus spake Tiresias and departed, leaving
his ivory stool despite his weight of years.

So Heracles, like a young plant in a garden,
was nurtured by his mother and known for the son
of Amphitryon the Argive. Apollo's son, the hero,
ancient Linus, was his unsleeping tutor
and taught the boy his letters; and Eurytus, the wealthy,   110
on account of the broad domains his fathers left him,
to bend the bow and speed the arrow home.
And Philammon's son, Eumolpus, made him a minstrel,
moulding both his hands to the boxwood lyre.
And all the tricks that Argive wrestlers use—
the movements from the legs, the swing of the buttocks—
to throw each other; and all the tricks of boxers,
devils with the thongs, and those of the all-in wrestlers,
who throw themselves on the ground, skills proper to their
     art:
all these he learned in tutelage to Hermes' son,   120
Harpalycus of Panopeus—and none who saw him from far
would confidently wait his turn to fight him;
upon his threatening eye sat such a scowl!
But to drive a chariot and horses, turn them safely
round the post, watching the nave of the wheel,
Amphitryon taught him himself, with a father's care;
for many a prize had he carried off for races
in the horse country of Argos: the unbroken cars
on which he used to stand, with time had all
slacked their straps. To reach with his spear while keeping   130
his shoulder under the shield as he sought his man,
to bear the sword's touch, to draw up lines
for battle, to size up an enemy party approaching,
to order horse, he learned of Hippalus' son,
Castor, exiled from Argos, all whose lands
and vineyards broad had Tydeus at Adrastus' hand
received, and dwelt in the horse country of Argos:

none other warrior was there among heroes
like to Castor, till age had frayed his youth.

140   Thus was Heracles reared by his loving mother;
but while a boy, his couch was by his father—
the skin of a lion, wherein he much delighted.
His dinner was roast meat, and a great loaf
of Dorian bread in a basket—enough to fill
a labouring man for sure. But during the day
his fare was slight and eaten cold. His tunic
was unadorned and barely reached the knee. . . .

❧Idyll XXVI

This short piece has assuredly been more of an enigma to scholars than even Idyll XII. It is composed of three parts, the last being a perfunctory invocation of Dionysus and the heroines of the tale. The first tells succinctly of the bloody end of Pentheus, king of Thebes, at the hands of three bands of maenads (female devotees of Bacchus), one of them led by his mother, Agave—the legend best known, to Theocritus as to us, as the plot of the *Bacchae* of Euripides, which in all essentials it resembles. In the second, the poet comments briefly on the tale and startles us by his uncompromising condemnation of the victim and exoneration of the god and his agents. That he expects to shock seems clear from his abrupt, half-defiant, half-shrugging disclaimer, as also from his repudiation at the outset of any contradiction—nor need we suppose that such an extreme solution of the moral dilemma exhibited by the tale would find ready acceptance among cultivated circles in his day. However, since this is almost certainly an early work, we have no means of knowing what readership he expected it to find, or whether indeed it was not written largely for personal motives. Besides the abrupt transitions (with which we may compare Idyll XII) there is a certain roughness in the versification, which nowhere approaches the best Theocritean standards, so that an early solution to the moral repugnance the poem excited was to suppose it falsely ascribed. This argument is unimpressive, especially since myths were traditionally treated by Greek poets as data on which to assert a position of identification with the gods,* and indeed Theocritus may appear to do the same thing in the Castor episode of Idyll XXIV. This very unoriginality perhaps reinforces the impression

---

*Dover, *Select Poems*, p. 264, gives several instances of a comparable sanctimony.

left by the composition that this is an early poem of Theocritus, while its audacity and power of narration unite to confirm that it is his. Its discovery in the Antinoan papyrus of ca. 500 A.D. tends also to favour its authenticity.

Various explanations of the poem's singularity have been offered, none entirely convincing, though two at least seem to shed some light: one that in the first part a picture is being described (we might compare Epigram III, though there the present tense is used, here the past); and the other that the whole is a reaction to reading (or seeing) Euripides' play. To the first we may concede that the representation is highly visual, but this may be scarcely to say more than 'highly Theocritean' (cf. the introduction to Idyll I); to the second that it is certainly unthinkable that perhaps the greatest, and certainly the most disturbing of the humanist playwright's works should not have provided the fuel for all subsequent moral questionings of the justice and responsibility of the powers that rule this world; indeed, his presentation of the Pentheus myth was the latest and most striking encapsulation of these questions for the Greek consciousness: they needs must arise directly from it. (So the *Bacchae*, along with other plays of Euripides, soon became, and long remained, a school text for rhetorical exercises—the equivalent of our written compositions on set subjects.)

In order to see what Theocritus is attempting to do with the myth, we may consider the respects in which his story differs from Euripides' play. Minor discrepancies in reporting the Bacchic ritual we may suppose to be details supplied in accordance with Hellenistic antiquarian taste and lore: the three *thiasoi*, or bands of maenads, with their three leaders; the virgin land chosen for the mysteries; the altars of turf, decked with leaves; the cult objects produced in secret from a chest and placed on the altars —concealed, it may be, by the leaves; the ritual nakedness of the women.* Euripides' account is altogether more general: Pentheus sees the maenads singing and mending their thyrsi (ritual

---

*In view of the ritual context, this seems the likeliest reason for the statement that they pulled their skirts out at the girdle to pursue Pentheus, though 'pulled out' is as ambiguous in the Greek as in English and could imply rather

wands of the Bacchic cult) in a wooded spot, which permits
him to observe them from a treetop, whereas Theocritus, who
has changed the location to open land, has him watch from a
crag, hidden behind a bush. His Pentheus, then, observes not
only the maenads, but their *arcana* (secret cult objects). Perhaps
Theocritus means to establish the propriety of expiation by
ritual sacrifice the more firmly by having him commit the clear-
est profanation—so giving the case the sharpest possible defini-
tion.

But the most striking respect in which Theocritus' account
differs from Euripides' is in the absence from the scene of Dio-
nysus. We meet only his votaries, who are acting under his in-
spiration. Euripides had been accused of atheism: is Theocritus
drawing out of him the extreme position that man is governed
by irrational forces without and within, to which the names of
gods have been given but which are responsible to no law and
render man equally irresponsible? It is perhaps unlikely that Eu-
ripides ever saw things in so starkly rationalistic a light, though
it seems sometimes to gleam upon his presentations. He was,
after all, a playwright, not a philosopher or rhetorician, and as
such was concerned to expose dramatically the world he per-
ceived, not to write its exposé. In Theocritus' poem, the moral
intention is explicit. To Euripides' 'See how the gods treat men'
he adds his apparently cynical 'And they have a perfect right to
behave as they will'. When confronted with the problem of the
rights of the gods, Greeks as widely diverse as Homer, Aeschy-
lus, Plato, and Epicurus had tended to assert that these were
subject to prior physical and moral laws—and physical and
moral in Greek thought tended to be assumed to each other.
Euripides in effect witnesses to this very law when he impugns
the gods for breaking it. If this implies a denial of their godhead,
it implies also belief in an ultimate principle of justice. Theo-
critus, on the other hand, is implying that, whatever be the

---

that the *peplos* was pulled *up* and out (over the girdle) to facilitate running
(rather than let down by pulling the girdle out, as I—and Gow—take it). Both
motives would be easy to parallel in Greek literature.

nature of these powers, there is no faulting them on moral grounds; their will *is* their right. However, neither here nor elsewhere (cf. Idyll I) does he go the length of admitting the transition to total humanism that his assumptions suggest. Though we may not wish to build much on the formal salutation to Dionysus, which looks like mere poetic decorum, yet purity and piety remain as binding on the man who hopes to be immune from disaster as they were on Aeschylus' Orestes or Sophocles' Oedipus. And though a cynic might suspect the Theocritean purity and piety to have been recast in a bourgeois mold as scrupulosity about rule and tradition out of a vague fear of the unknown, yet man's respect for the powers that rule him is seen as somehow linked with a Zeus who requites. So that while it may seem that Theocritus' world is more hostile to man than that of Euripides, insofar as man cannot even appeal to a higher law to convict the gods of injustice, yet it is perhaps less hostile than that of Sophocles' *Oedipus Tyrannus*, since it is men, and not the gods or fate, who rule their own destiny. Or do they? Recalling other poems, such as Idyll I, we may wonder whether Theocritus is not still half aware of the Oedipean pitfall — whether the aspiration to purity is not half resolve and half prayer. However, the maxim that closes this section is 'positively' Aeschylean (or Pindaric) in its assertion of the principle of nemesis: and Aeschylus' world view is notably less fatalistic than Sophocles'.

I see no reason to doubt that Theocritus' 'Bacchae' is an early work of its author. Indeed I find it alluring to regard it as a juvenile work composed under the stimulus of a first encounter with Euripides and the moral dilemma he invokes. Imagine a youthful version of the moderate-minded, ease-loving, but imaginative Simichidas of Idyll VII, horror-struck at the moral abyss uncovered before his civilized eyes, and stung to employ his newly assumed art in a forceful, and not altogether unsuccessful, rebuttal of the charge against the god of a tradition he has learned to revere if only for art's sake—and yet in the very attempt betraying himself as imbued with his age's own brand of post-Euripidean unbelief: its hollow homage to the forms of religion, combined with a reduction of the nonhuman import of the myths.

Alas, this boyhood Theocritus, engaging though I hope he may prove to others besides me, remains in a realm of inference. What I would urge as the only plausible explanation of the strange lines following his rejection of all criticism of the god is that the poet has some *actual* boy closely in mind. The reference to the eagle has excited in scholars some wild conjectures which need not be expounded here, but all unremarked has gone the significance, in the context, of a little-known myth, according to which the boy who in Zeus' own boyhood first did him homage was metamorphosed into the first eagle.* Now Theocritus, as his next line makes plain, is pointing to the honour that accrues to piety and also (an article of traditional faith) to the transmission of this honour through successive generations. The race of eagles continues to embody the reward of piety merited by its founding ancestor. And the fact that the ancestor was a boy makes this legend a peculiarly fitting illustration for an admonition to piety delivered to one in his tenth year.

Another tempting hypothesis is that the boy for whom the poem is written is the poet's own son. We know nothing of any children of Theocritus, but in view of our total lack of information about him, that is no argument that he had none, and it would still allow for an early date in his career as poet. It may be worth noting in passing that in this event the figure of Agave takes on an added significance as illustrating the poet's stance of acquiescence toward vengeance on the impious even if exacted by a parent on his child. But this guess, too, remains strictly outside the sphere of legitimate inference. That the poem is written for a boy, however, seems to me an adequate explanation of its peculiarities. For it serves also to illumine the blunt manner both of telling the tale and pointing the moral. Moreover, the 'heroic' invocation of Dionysus, while it gives practical illustration of the poet's precept of respect for traditional forms of

*Cited by Gow, p. 482.

piety, has an air of oddity understandable if the poet is deliberately conforming to school canons for correct composition of verses. Finally, it is pertinent to observe that the very choice of a sensational, not to say gory legend happens to coincide with the abiding literary tastes of boys!

The Bacchants

Ino and Autonoë and white-cheeked Agave
went as the leaders three of three bands to Cithaeron.
And some plucked the wild leaves from a tousled oak,
with ivy live, and the asphodel of the upper earth,
and in a virgin meadow raised up altars twelve:
three for Semele and nine for Dionysus.
Then handling out of a chest sacred things they had
  wrought,
in reverent silence laid them on the new-cut altars,
as Dionysus taught them, himself their inspiration.
But Pentheus watched all their deeds from a lofty crag,   10
hid in an ancient mastic tree that grew thereby.
Autonoë first saw him, and uttered a dreadful cry,
and straightway overturned with her feet the mystic things
of madding Bacchus, which the profane may not set eyes
  on,
and charged. Maddened she was, and straight were the
  others maddened.
Pentheus fled in fear, and they pursued him, pulling
their robes out at the girdle, a length to cover their thighs.
Then said Pentheus, 'What will you with me, women?'
And said Autonoë: 'You shall sooner know than hear.'
Then his mother seized the head of her child, and
  bellowed—   20
such a sound emits a lioness newly whelped—
and Ino tore off his great shoulder, blade and all,
placing her heel in his belly. Autonoë did likewise,
while the other women parted his other members among
  them.
And so to Thebes they came, spattered all with his blood,
and bringing from Cithaeron Penthema, not Penthea.*

*i.e., Mourning (*Penthēma*), not Pentheus (of which *Penthēa* is in Greek
the objective case).

I have no objection, nor let another concern him
for a foe of Dionysus—not if he suffer worse:
though he were in his ninth, or approaching his tenth year.
30   For myself, let me be pure, and to the pure found pleasing:
so has the eagle honour from aegis-bearing Zeus.
The children of pious men prosper, not those of the
    impious.

I give greeting to Dionysus, whom the All High set down
on snowy Dracanus, after he opened his mighty thigh.
And I greet fair Semele, and her sisters, Cadmeians loved
by many a dame, who did this deed all guiltless, moved
by Dionysus. Let none blame the acts of gods!

✿Idyll XXVIII

This charming dedicatory poem explains itself in the main. It was composed in the Lesbian dialect and in a metre favoured by Sappho, who treated it as a (rather loose) couplet. Theocritus' poem shows an odd number of lines, one of which appears, on grounds of style and content, superfluous. I have thought good to disencumber my English version of it and render the whole in loosely rhyming couplets, appropriate to so occasional a piece.

The Nicias to whose wife, Theugenis, the distaff is being presented is our old friend the doctor-poet of Idylls XI and XIII, and also of Epigram VIII. (See also General Introduction, p. 10, where the matter of the chronology of this poem is raised.)

It is perhaps helpful to add some factual notes. A distaff is an implement for spinning yarn and its invention is attributed to 'green-eyed' Pallas Athene, the warrior maiden, patroness of household crafts and all nonreproductive roles of women. The city founded by Nilus is Miletus, that by Archias Syracuse. The boast of Syracusan workmanship must have conjured up, for Theocritus' world, something of the sophistication until recently associated with Paris in ours. In stating that he is a native of Sicily, Theocritus in this poem provides us with a unique auto-biographical datum which at least gives credence to the tradition that claimed him for Syracuse (Cf. General Introduction, p. 9).

The Distaff

Distaff, friend of those who spin:
given to all wise women
who will o'er their households queen
first by her whose eyes are green:
be not loth to go with me
e'en to Nilus' famed city.
Zeus we'll ask a gracious wind
thither, that my friend may find
in our meeting every bliss
10   and return me kiss for kiss—
Nicias, the holy shoot
of the Muses, singers sweet.
You, of much-wrought ivory made,
in his wife's hands shall be laid
and work her many a work—the rough
garb of men, and women's stuff,
sheer as water. Theugenis
of the well-turned ankle is
such a wife as would the dams,
20   in the pastures with their lambs,
shorn of their soft fleeces were,
in her service, twice a year;
for as busy as the bee
and as provident is she.
Nor had you been sent to one
feeble-fingered or a drone;
for your native city was
colonized by Archias
of Ephyra, heart of the
30   famous isle of Sicily;
so you are my countryman,
now to home with one who can
cure with drugs and make men well.
Mid Ionians you shall dwell,

in Miletus of fair fame.
Theugenis shall have the name
of the best bespindled wife,
to remind her all her life
of her poetry-loving friend.
All who see you shall commend   40
grace so great in gift so small,
saying, 'Friendship riches all.'

✿Idylls XXIX & XXX

The two following poems likewise need little elucidation. Their appeal to the reader—allowance being made for the homosexual convention of Greek love—is direct and their beauty may be left to work upon him so far as the translation permits. Theocritus —somewhat in the manner exaggerated by Simichidas in Idyll VII—has a strikingly direct approach to his own love affairs, surrounding them neither with sentiment nor with disgust but merely with the bittersweetness of a half-hope of felicity resigning itself to continual frustration. The poems may serve to arouse our sympathies for the predicament of a man of culture and sensibility in a world where the earthly love partner, woman, was normally his social and intellectual inferior, and God at best a formidably remote object for even Platonic, sublimated eros. In particular, the second poem displays a fatalism that is saved from cynicism by being so much more human a thing—the sigh of one on whom age has begun to weigh, as he prepares to submit not gracelessly to the necessity, as he sees it, of the tyrant Eros. The disillusionment of the first poem is less general: it is the boy who is rebuked for fickleness and the weather eye he has for his social betterment.* The yoke, it seems, is still borne willingly.

Written in Sapphic metres and the Lesbian dialect traditional to love poetry (the opening line of Idyll XXIX is a quotation from Alcaeus), both compositions would seem to belong to the period, roughly speaking, of Idyll XXVIII, and on internal grounds to a later era than Idyll XII, which is by comparison naively optimistic. (See also the introductions to Idylls II and XII, General Introduction, pp. 10–11.)

*This is my interpretation of what Gow, p. 507, concedes to be the "desperate difficulties" posed by ll. 20–22.

Lines to a Boy, I

Wine, dear boy, it is said, and Truth go together:
then we too should be truthful when in our cups.
I shall declare what lingers in the furthest
corner of my mind; thus: that you will not love me
with all your heart. I know it, for half my life
is mine by reason of your beauty; the rest has perished.
And when you will, my day is like to the immortals',
and when you are unwilling, much in darkness.
Can it be fitting, thus to betray to grief
your lover? If you would pay some heed to me,   10
who am the older man, while you are young,
you would profit yourself thereby and own me right.
Make for yourself one nest, in a single tree,
where comes no preying serpent. As things are,
today you perch on a bough, tomorrow another,
and change from this to that. Whoever sees
and praises your fair face, you have become
straightway his friend of more than three years' standing;
while he who loved you first is placed among
your acquaintance of three days! This smells to me   20
of men of vain ambition. Long as you live,
let your love be loyal and for your equal.
This if you do, you will win the praise of your townsmen,
and even Eros could not ride you hard,
though readily he subdues the minds of men
and has made of me a weakling, out of iron!
I entreat you, by your tender mouth, recall
you yesteryear were younger than you are,
and old we grow and wrinkled ere we spit!
Nor may it be we have our youth again,   30
who bears wings on his shoulders. We are slow
to catch at flying things! So, thinking thus
should make you tread more softly, love in return
your lover without guile; that when you wear
the beard of manhood on your cheeks, we'll be

Achilles and his friend to one another.
But if you cast my words upon the wind
and say in your heart, 'Why do you vex me, sir?'
Though now I'd travel after the golden apples
40   on your account, or fetch the ward of the dead,
Cerberus—then, though you called me, I'd not stir
so far as the door, my grief and longing over.

Lines to a Boy, II

Alas for this dire complaint, it bodes no good!
For two months now a quartan love attacks me,
for a boy only passably handsome—yet every inch
he stands above the ground is grace surpassing,
and the charm of the smile on his cheeks. . . . And now the
    mischief:
some days it claims me, some days lets me be,
and soon I shall find no peace even for sleep.
For yesterday he gave me a slight glance
from under his eyelids as he passed—too bashful
10   to look me in the face—and his skin grew rosy.
Then Eros took a tighter hold on my heart,
and home I went, nursing this fresh sore.
So calling on my soul, I had my say with myself:
'What are you doing again? What end to this folly?
Has it not been borne in on you yet that the hairs
on your temples are grey? It is time you had learned to be
    prudent.
Your looks are far from young; then do not act
for all like those who newly savour their years.
And another thing you forget; that better it were
20   for an older man to make strange to a love that's cruel.
For a boy's life goes on, like the generations
of the swift deer: tomorrow he'll loose his tackle
and sail in another direction; and the sweet flower
of his youth abides with him, as with those of like age.

To the other is left desire, which gnaws at his marrow,
as he feeds on memories; and many a vision
haunts him by night. A year will not suffice
to rid him of his sickness.' These arguments,
and many another, I used to upbraid my soul;
but she replied, 'Whoever thinks to conquer   30
scheming Eros, as well may think to find
how many times nine are the stars above us!'
And now, if I will, I must make me a long neck
to draw the yoke, an if I will not; for this, sir,
is the god's decision who cheated the mighty mind
of Zeus, and even the Cyprian herself. Ah, me,
a passing leaf, wanting but little wind,
he'll swiftly seize and bear away with his blast!

Fragment of *Berenice*
Epigrams

❧Fragment of *Berenice*

A fragment of another poem by Theocritus is cited by Athenaeus (7.284A) in the second century A.D. I here translate the whole passage:

> Theocritus the Syracusan, in the poem called *Berenice*, calls the fish named Leukos [literally, 'White'] 'holy', in the following lines:

> And if a fisherman should ask abundant
> booty from the sea whereby he lives—
> his nets his ploughshares—and at fall of night
> a holy fish should slaughter to this goddess—
> that men call Leukos, holiest of fishes—
> he'd spread his net and draw it from the brine
> brimful. . . .

Much later Eustathius, in his commentary on the *Iliad*, mentions the same passage (at *Iliad* 16.407), which he presumably only knows from Athenaeus. Nothing more is known about the poem. Clearly the goddess referred to is Berenice herself, so that a probable conjecture is that it relates to the deification of the mother of Ptolemy II and Arsinoë II (compare my introduction to Idyll XVII).

&Epigrams

The collection of epigrams ascribed to Theocritus, which is
found in two manuscript traditions and in the Palatine An-
thology, appears to have been made late and from scattered
inscriptions and other material. It is lacking in the collection
known as Meleager's Garland (first century B.C.), from which
we have most of Callimachus' epigrams. I have translated them
all because it is impossible to assert or deny with certitude the
authenticity of the ascription to Theocritus of any one of them.
Epigram VIII may reasonably be taken to be addressed to the
Doctor Nicias of Idylls IX, XIII, and XXVIII and to have been
presented by Theocritus to his old friend for inscription on a
statue of the latter's patron god Asclepius. Epigram XIII is of the
same type. Epigram V is too Theocritean to be true—in fact a
pastiche. Epigram III might seem to have the authentic inventive
ring. Epigrams VI and XVI display a suffering sensitivity, almost
a morbidity, in the face of death which seems un-Theocritean,
and yet must be ascribed to a powerful poetic genius. The Pala-
tine Anthology gives Leonidas of Tarentum as the author of XVI
(and also of VII, XIX, XI, and XX), and this is certainly plausible
(for Leonidas, see the introduction to Idyll VII).

The collection of epigrams falls broadly speaking into three
classes: 1) inscriptions for pictures (as III, V, VI) or statues (VIII, X,
XIII), often specifically of cult objects or offerings at shrines (I, II,
III, XI, XXIV); 2) inscriptions for or from gravestones (VII, IX, XI,
XV, XVI, XX, XXIII); 3) the virtuoso pieces in different metres,
some commemorating the poets whose names are associated
with them, which are very probably from the hand of Theo-
critus, who already displays the scope of his metrical versatility
in the *Idylls*, and intended for or copied from statues of the poets
(XVI–XIX, XXI, XXII). It seems probable that XX became included

[210]

on account of its striking metre and it is unlikely to be by Theo-
critus, as is the oddity XIV, of which the function appears clearly
enough—as indeed is generally the case with the Epigrams.

Note on the metres. In Epigrams XIX, XX, and XXI, I have given
syllabic and stress equivalents of the metres of the originals,
since these are in the main the characteristic metres of the poets
celebrated, and are named for them. In Epigrams XVIII and XXIV
I have more generally suggested the form of the Greek verse.
The majority of the remaining poems I have represented by
rhymed English verse, usually of five stresses.

I

These dewy roses and that clustered thyme
are offerings to the Heliconian Nine;
but these dark-leavèd laurels, they are thine,
O Pythian Paean; for thy Delphian fane
so decks herself to please thee. And thy shrine
yon hornèd goat, the white, shall redly stain—
now nibbling on a branch of turpentine.

II

To Pan the white-skinned Daphnis—he who plays,
upon his darling pipes, bucolic lays—
offers his piercèd reeds, his club, sharp spear,
fawnskin, and apple-scrip of yesteryear.

III

Daphnis, you sleep upon the leaf-strewn soil,
resting your body, heavy all with toil.
The hillside bristles with your stakes new-set;
but others are awake and hunting yet:
Pan and Priapus, who is fixing brave
his brow with golden ivy. To the cave

they stalk in concert, and you lying there. . . .
Ah, leave your sleep and fly their more insensate snare!

IV

Goatherd, the windings of that lane pursue,
there by the oaks, to a newly carved statue,
of figwood, bark and all; he's legless, earless,
but by no means impotent; his fertile phallus
can do the Cyprian's work. There lies around
a holy precinct, where from rocks a gush
of deathless waters burgeons, laurels spring
with scented cypress tree and myrtle bush,
and thereabouts a vine goes spiralling
and pours its fruitful burden on the ground.
His clear-toned melody the blackbird shrills,
and all of spring is in his fluted grace notes;
while golden nightingales resound in trills
the honied strainings of articulate throats.
There sit you down: say to fair Priapus,
if he relieve me of my lust for Daphnis,
straight I will sacrifice a pretty kid.
If he refuse, but I obtain my end,
I'll offer triple sacrifice—I'll send
him heifer, hairy goat, and lamb stall-fed.
Go, and may the god with favour hear you.

V

Pray, by the nymphs, will you on your double reeds
pipe to me something soothing? I'll tune up
my lyre and start some music from its strings,
while Cowherd Daphnis, by the modulation
of wax-bound breath, shall charm us both. Let's stand
beside the leafy oak, behind his cave,
and rob old nanny-riding Pan of sleep!

VI

Ah, you sad Thyrsis, what more can you, though
you melt your two eyes weeping in your grief?
The kid is gone, your pretty wean—she's gone
to Hades; the cruel wolf crushed her in his teeth.
The dogs are baying, but you, what more can you?
Nor bone nor ash is left of her—she's gone.

VII

An infant son you left, and your own prime,
when you quit living and acquired this tomb,
Eurymedon! With heroes now your home;
and him will every citizen esteem,
remembering his father's goodly fame.

VIII

To Miletus now is come
none other than the son of Paean;
with a man to live at one,
Nicias the physician,
who never ceases him to pray,
burning incense, day by day.
So he had this carving done
from fragrant cedar. Eëtion
he had promised a large sum—
all whose skill was lavished on
the master hand's conception.

IX

You who pass by, a man of Syracuse,
Orthon, gives you warning: never use
excess of liquor on a stormy night,
which was the reason of my present plight.
See how, my glorious birthplace far away,
I lie investitured in foreign clay!

X

Goddesses, to delight all nine of you,
Xenocles set up this marble statue.
He has the Muses' gift, as all agree;
and for this fame holds them in memory.

XI

For Eusthenes the physiognomer
this monument. He could the character
tell even from the eye, he was so clever.
On foreign soil he lies, a foreigner.
His friends have given him decent burial—
the poet very much their friend withal.
The master, dead, received all honour due,
and in his helplessness found bearers true.

XII

Demomenes the Choregus,
who set up, Dionysus,
sweetest of gods, to you,
this tripod and statue,
observed in everything
the Mean. With the men's chorus
he won the prize, by focussing
on the Beautiful and the Due.

XIII

No Common Cypris this. Propitiate her
as Heaven-born. The chaste Chrysogone set her
in Amphicles his house, in life her partner
as in their offspring. Lady, as they ever
began with you, so each year saw them prosper;
for, caring for the gods, menselves do better.

XIV

This bank alike serves citizen and strange.
Place and withdraw; we keep the reckoning right.
Be others chary? Caicus will change
your foreign notes to order, even at night.

XV

You who pass by, whether you bestow
more on the brave than on the coward I'll know,
when you shall call a blessing on this gravestone;
for light it lies on the head of Eurymedon.

XVI

This child untimely went to Hades, ere
her age could ripen, in her seventh year,
mourning her loss—a twenty-month-old brother,
who tasted loveless death ere he had speech.
Ah, Peristere, piteously who suffer:
how much of pain have gods set in men's reach!

XVII

Stranger, look on this statue and admire,
and say, when home art come, 'In Teos I saw
an image of Anacreon, the greatest
of ancient lyric poets.' When thou addest,
'In youths was his delight and his desire,'
thou wilt narrate the whole man, without flaw.

XVIII

The speech is Dorian,
and Doric, too, the man,
Epicharmus,
inventor of Comedy.
We, O Bacchus,

dwellers of the mighty
Syracusan city,
offer him you,
a citizen from our ranks,
but bronze, not true.
Gratitude is but fit,
as we recall his wit,
and many a truth
serviceable to our youth.
To him great thanks.

XIX

(scazon, or 'limping' measure)
Here lies the master limping poet, Hipponax;
So if perchance you are a rogue, you'll please keep back.
But if you're honest and your folks of wholesome stuff,
No problem—sit you down and, if you like, doze off!

XX

(hendecasyllable plus Archilochian)
This memorial little Medius has
set by the road for his nurse, a Thracian, and inscribed it 'Cleite'.
Thus shall she have received her compensation
for that she nurtured him. How? In that still she'll be known for
    faithful service.

XXI

*(Archilochian plus iambic trimeter acatalectic plus iambic trimeter
    catalectic)*
Stand you and look on Archilochus, poet of old, the man of
    Satire,
whose glory manifold has spread through all the earth:
to western shore of night, and eastward to the morning:

Certain it is that the Muses and Delian Apollo loved him, that
    he
so musical became, so skilled at making verse,
so masterly at scoring words for lyre and singer.

XXII

This is the first of poets who of old
of Heracles, the son of Zeus, have told,
the lion-fighter and the swift of hand:
Pisander is he, of Camirus, and
he all the toils he had to undergo
related. That you may the better know,
his fellow townsmen have in bronze set here
himself, though after many a month and year.

XXIII

Whose grave is this? Who lies beneath this stone?
Glauce's the grave, and name by which she's known.

XXIV

The offerings Apollo's were of old;
the base below is younger by amounts
that vary: some by seven years, or five,
some twelve, and some two hundred. The accounts
produced these figures when their tale was told.

Appendix
Bibliography
Index

❧ Appendix

Why Idylls VIII, IX, XIX, XX, XXI, XXIII, XXV, and XXVII are regarded as spurious works of Theocritus is a question that must have been posed by many readers, who so far have been referred to the judgment of Gow (Translator's Preface, p. viii). A little more specific information is appended here, with particular consideration of the three poems among them (VIII, IX, and XXV) whose Theocritean pretensions are the hardest to dismiss.

In a general manner, as far as the manuscript tradition is concerned, the whole collection hangs together, though there are some important qualifications to this statement. Thus only VIII is with certainty to be found in the papyri which form our oldest records and go back as far as the second century A.D.—a mere half millenium after Theocritus himself, and (be it noted) later than Virgil's *Eclogues* with their many Theocritean echoes. Only VIII and IX are in what I have stated elsewhere to be 'incontrovertibly the best manuscript tradition, that represented by the Ambrosian Codex K' (thirteenth century). For the rest, which appear in one or two inferior manuscripts at best, the ascription to Theocritus is of far less weight, or, in the cases of XXIII and XXVII, of none (see Gow's introductions to the individual poems).

The authenticity of all these pieces has further been disputed on grounds of linguistic usage, dialect, metre, and style in general—considerations of their nature inconclusive since they raise questions as to how far the author may have varied his usage under different influences or at different times. Of more substance are considerations of subject, treatment, and general tone, since these invite comparison with other authors and periods, particularly later ones. On such grounds XIX, XX, XXIII, and XXVII—all love poems, though of very differing themes—are

generally ascribed to a later epoch. Of the rest, XXI is qualita-
tively outstanding, but idiosyncratic by any Greek standard;
concerning itself to display the hard lives of poor fishermen, it is
reminiscent in its realism of the Wordsworth of *Michael* and in
no way of Theocritus as he is known to us.

Of the remaining three poems, two (VIII and IX) are bucolic,
XXV is an epic in miniature (see introductions to Idylls XIII and
XXII), subdivided into three episodes (the titles of the first two
are in the manuscripts, though this does not guarantee that they
are by the original author) all relating to two well-known La-
bours of Heracles: the cleaning of the stables of Augeas by diver-
sion of the stream Menius (1. 13), and the killing of the Lion of
Nemea. These are all treated in the oblique manner generally
favoured by Callimachus and his following, and perhaps by
Theocritus himself; however, his extant epyllia, the *Hylas* (XIII),
Dioscuri (XXII), and *Baby Heracles* (XXIV), all narrate their adven-
tures directly, whereas Idyll XXV devotes its first two episodes
entirely to matter peripheral to Augeas and his stables and in its
third gives the story of the lion-slaying through the narration of
Heracles.

I offer translations of these three poems, partly in order to
have discharged to the fullest possible extent—or rather beyond
it—my claim to have translated Theocritus into English verse,
partly to enable the reader to make comparison with the poems
reliably ascribed to him. The close reader of Gow will discover
that he displays some reluctance entirely to dismiss the possi-
bility that VIII and XXV might be of Theocritus' authorship. Idyll
IX he regards as inferior and un-Theocritean—a judgment in
which I cannot wholly concur. It is worthy of note too—though
it proves nothing as to authenticity—that Virgil has close imita-
tions of Idylls VIII and IX in his third and seventh Eclogues. It
is likely—though unprovable—that he regarded them as by
Theocritus, as they continued to be regarded for succeeding
centuries down to the last.

In inviting comparison of the epyllion, XXV, with Idylls XIII,
XXII (to which it perhaps bears the most resemblance), and XXIV,
it should be mentioned that the Greek idiom is much more

'Homeric' than in any of these—though as noted above, this is in itself hardly a good argument against authorship. I may state in a general way that I find both Idylls VIII and XXV to be lacking in the fertile inventiveness (what the Romans called *inventio*) of Theocritus' genuine pieces, as of all first-rate poetry. (Indeed, they may serve to point up that pre-eminent quality of both his bucolic and epic verse.) Idyll VIII contains nothing but standard bucolic themes revolving round the herdsman's life and loves. Gow too remarks of it that 'the setting of the songs certainly has the air of being modelled on *Idd* 5 and 6, and if all are by T., he has shown some poverty of invention' (p. 170). Idyll XXV is low-keyed for over two-hundred lines—even where Heracles is charged by the bull—though there are pleasant enough passages, including the delightful *Odyssey*-like exclamation of the old ploughman over the behaviour of dogs: competent and interesting work, but lacking Theocritus' imaginative quality. Even the lengthy and detailed account of the overcoming of the lion, with its Homeric simile of the bending of the figwood shoots, lacks the excitement and relish of the overcoming of Amycus in Idyll XXII.

It is otherwise with IX, where, in the unexpected turns that the poet gives to the theme—particularly at the ends of sections —the inventiveness is striking: one might say startling in the instance of the heifers blown off the cliff: thus the similes that round off the songs of both Daphnis and Menalcas, the picturesque means of illustrating the uncommon size of the shell, and the curiously morbid note struck at the end of the concluding eulogy of Muse and song by the evocation of Circe's poisoned cup. (Cf. the ending of Idyll VII and my Introduction, p. 88).

Moreover, in IX, attitudes and turns of expression several times suggest *in a general way* the genuine works of Theocritus. Thus Menalcas' song could be a prototype of that of the Cyclops in Idyll XI, and especially for lines 42–50; the blisters on the tongue of line 31—explained by the Scholiast as denoting a debt unpaid—recall the warts on the nose of Idyll XII; the mode of expression of lines 31–32 recalls lines 30–31 in Idyll X and also lines 3–7 in Idyll XII, while the sentiment of lines 31–36 generally suggests the quality of Theocritus' feeling for Grace and Muse in Idyll XVI.

Such general reminiscences are far better evidence in favour of authenticity than verbal ones, which immediately raise the suspicion of imitation. That Idyll IX is at times—and especially in its first half—maladroit is undeniable. I am not convinced that this clumsiness, either of content, wording, or metre, is sufficient to compel agreement with those critics who have rejected the opening section as spurious while assigning what follows to Theocritus, or to conclude with Cholmeley that 'the poem began, therefore, withoưt introduction'. I am inclined to view Idyll IX as a very early essay by Theocritus in the bucolic mode, in which we glimpse some of the themes and mannerisms which reappear more elaborately and convincingly handled in his mature work. My reading of the concluding section—also sometimes amputated by critics—tends to support this view and is dealt with in a note to my translation.

A tantalizing point remains to be raised which relates to posterity's claim upon Theocritus as the 'Father of Pastoral'. (See General Introduction, pp. 11–14.) With the exception of the mime, number II in our collection, and of IV, Idylls I–XI all show us samples of the bucolic 'song within' (see General Introduction, p. 12). Of these, Idylls V, VI, VII, (VIII), and now IX set one song against another, but with thematic variations. In V the songs demonstrate the bitter opposition of the singers; in VI their equal creativity as singers, fitting them for reconciliation in love; in VII (a very complex poem, be it recalled) two modes of poetic composition, with the idyllic mastery of the one poet, the aspiring tutelage of the other. Idyll IX recalls VI in the equality of the singers, but the love motif is missing. Only in VIII are we presented with what we must deduce to be the prototype situation: that hypothetically based on the country custom of the singing match, with two singers, two straightforward songs (not the thinly disguised invective of V), and an umpire who makes the award to one—and that the archetypal Daphnis—to the discomfiture of the other. We must suppose this to have been, from the genre's outset, the commonest form, offering scope and variety in the free invention of the 'songs within' rather than in the accompanying situations, which seems likely to be a secondary and later development. Idyll VIII appears as a rather commonplace—though certainly quite accomplished— exemplar of this 'primary mode'; it could even have got itself included in our collection on the grounds that Theocritus must have composed such pieces. If it is by him, we must suppose it early and rendered sterile by an existing convention unsuited to his true talents and awaiting the impetus of these to break its bonds.

Idyll VIII

Herdsmen

The graceful Daphnis, minding his herd on the hillsides,
was met, so they say, by Menalcas tending his flock:
both were ruddy of head and beardless both;
both were skilled on the flute and both at singing.
Now Menalcas first to Daphnis said when he saw him:
'Daphnis, ward of lowing kine, are you willing
to sing me a match? I warrant I will o'ercome you,
an I sing all I have in mind'. To this Daphnis answered:
'Shepherd of woolly sheep, piper Menalcas,
10   never shall you o'ercome me: sing till you burst!'

MENALCAS
Are you willing to see? Are you willing to lay a stake?

DAPHNIS
I am willing to see. I am willing to lay a stake.

MENALCAS
What now shall we lay? What that befits us both?

DAPHNIS
I'll lay a calf; you a lamb big as its mother.

MENALCAS
Never a lamb lay I, for my father is strict
and my mother: at evening they count the whole flock.

DAPHNIS
Then what do you lay? The victor must have his advantage.

MENALCAS
I've a fine pipe that I made of nine reeds:
the wax is white and even, above and below;
20   that I could lay: my father's goods will I not.

DAPHNIS

In sooth, I too have a nine-reed pipe:
the wax is white and even, above and below;
but lately I put it together: my finger still smarts
here, where the reed, when I split it, cut back at me!

MENALCAS

Who shall judge between us? Who give ear to our singing?

DAPHNIS

We could call, maybe, that goatherd there—do you see
  him?
whose dog, with the white muzzle, barks at the kids.

So the boys called, and the goatherd heeded and came;
and the boys sang, and the goatherd agreed to be judge.
So first, as the lot fell, sang Cryer Menalcas;   30
then Daphnis took up the interweaving strain,
country-style. Menalcas thus began:

MENALCAS

Groves and rivers, race of gods, if ever
        Piper Menalcas pleased you with his song,
feed with a will my lambs, and if his calves
        Daphnis should bring, no less grant him.

DAPHNIS

Fountains and fallows, springing to delight, if truly
        Daphnis sings songs like the nightingales,
fatten this herd, and if Menalcas lead
        aught hither, in all plenty may he joy!   40

MENALCAS

There sheep, there goats twin-bearing, and there bees
        fill the hives; there the oaks are higher:
there walks fair Milon by; if he depart,
        parched yon shepherd, parched the fallows.

DAPHNIS
Everywhere Spring, everywhere herds; their udders
      gush with milk and so their young are fed.
And there fair Naïs roams; if she depart,
      the cattle and the cowherd both are dry.

MENALCAS
Go you, mate of the white she-goats, to the forest's
50   heart—here, snub-nosed kids, to the water!—
There you'll find him. Tell him, Stumpy, 'Milon,
      Proteus, though a god, was herd to seals!'

DAPHNIS
Trees dread the winter, streams the drought,
      birds the snare, wild things the net, and man
desire for a soft maid. O Father, Zeus,
      not alone am woman-lover I!

And thus the children through exchanges sang.
The final round Menalcas thus began:

MENALCAS
Spare my kids; spare, wolf, my dams; do me
60   no harm, though small I be and shepherd many.
My dog, Lampurus, deep asleep? You should not,
while herding with a child, so deeply slumber.
My ewes, shrink not to sate yourselves with tender
grass; 'twill grow again ere you shall want.
Go graze you, graze you! Fill your udders all,
that part the lambs may have, part I for cheeses.

Then Daphnis in turn lifted his clear voice up:

DAPHNIS
A maid with meeting brows spied on me yesterday
from the cave as I drove my heifers past, and called me
70   'Handsome! Handsome!' Not even a jeering answer

I gave her, but followed my way with downcast eyes.
Sweet the voice of the heifer, sweet her breath;
sweet by streams to couch from summer's heat.
As acorns adorn the oak and apples their tree,
so the calf the cow, and his very cattle the cowherd.

So sang the boys, and thus the goatherd spoke:
'Sweet is your verse, Daphnis, exquisite your notes.
I had rather hear you make music than sup on honey.
Take the pipes; in singing you have o'ercome.
But if you are willing to teach me somewhat myself,   80
as I tend my goats alongside, I will give you
that hornless goat as your fee; she always fills
the bucket over the brim'. So the boy rejoiced,
leaping and clapping his hands at his win, as a kid
leaps by its mother. The other smarted, his mind
o'erthrown by grief, as sorrows a maid deflowered.
Thereafter was Daphnis first among herdsmen, and scarce
his boyhood past, he married the nymph Naïs.

Idyll IX

Daphnis and Menalcas

Sing roundels, Daphnis; do you begin the songs;
begin, Daphnis; let Menalcas follow.
Put the calves to suck; let in the bulls
to the calfless cows: let them graze together
and roam among the flowers, not scorning the herd.
Do you sing rounds for me upon the one side
and from the other Menalcas make reply.

DAPHNIS
Sweet is the heifer's voice and sweet the cow's;
sweet the pipe and the herdsman; sweet sing I.
10　My bed is beside the cool water, heaped
with fine skins from my white heifers—swept
from the cliff by the South Wind, as they nibbled arbutus.
I care as much for summer's scorch as lovers
care to hear father or mother prate!

Thus sang Daphnis to me, and thus Menalcas:

MENALCAS
My mother is Etna. I too dwell snug, in a cave
in her hollow rocks. I have wealth such as men dream of:
sheep in plenty, goats in plenty; their skins
lie at my head and feet. On the fire of oak,
20　sausages sizzle, on the fire acorns roast
in winter. Truly to winter I pay as much heed
as the toothless man to nuts when wheatcake's by!

I applauded and straightway gave them a prize: to Daphnis
a stave which my father's field put forth—a growth
a carpenter might not despise; to the other a shell,
a graceful whorl I caught on the Icaran rocks,

and on its meat I fed myself, having cut it
in five for five. And he sounded the hollow shell.

Country Muses, a fair farewell: make known
the songs that once I heard* among these herdsmen.   30
No longer may the tip of my tongue grow blisters.
Cricket to cricket is dear, ant to ant
and hawk to hawk: so to me is Muse and song.
May all my house be full of her; sweeter is not
sleep, nor sudden Spring, nor flowers to bees:
so dear to me are the Muses. Those they look
upon in love not Circe's cup can harm!

*Here a very slight emendation of the Greek text—'heard' (*ākousa*) for
'sang' (*aeisa*)—makes sense of the whole, so that there is no reason to reject
this closing section or (with Gow) to put the concluding six lines into quota-
tion marks and regard them as in themselves a 'song' (that referred to in l. 30,
where I have adopted the inferior MS reading, 'songs')—which they plainly
are not! This solution of the problem of these lines was hit upon by my
husband, John M. Rist, during the latest (and last?) of the 'Theocritean con-
frontations' referred to in my Preface.

Idyll XXV

Heracles the Lion-Slayer

Heracles and the Countryman

Him the ancient, the ploughman and tender of cattle addressed,
breaking off the task he had in hand. 'My friend,
gladly will I tell you all that you ask, for I stand
in awe of the dread eye of Hermes God of the Roads—
most wrathful of the gods, they say, should one refuse
a traveller seeking to know the way. Now the fleecy flocks
of King Augeas do not all feed in one pasture
or single spot, but some on the banks surrounding the swift
Helisus, some by divine Alphaeus' sacred stream;
10   some toward the vineyards of Bouprasion; some are here.
But for all the cattle, utterly teeming as they are,
these grazing-grounds flourish yearlong throughout
the Menius' great demesnes; from under their dews the meadows
and pastures put forth honied grass enough to raise
a mighty strain of horned cattle. Their stalls are here
to your right: the whole is plainly seen from the other side
of the flowing river, there where the plane trees grow in stands
and the paler olives—the spot, my friend, is consecrate
to Apollo the Herdsman, a very powerful god. Hard by
20   have been constructed the long huts for the labourers, we
who duly gather in wealth untold for our king,
casting the seed in furrows turned thrice and even four times.
As to the bounds, they are known to the toiling cultivators
who come to the winepresses when vintage time is here.
For this whole plain belongs to wise Augeas, all
its dark furrows and leafy groves, as far as the farthest
pine-dressed mountain spine, and we cross it all day long
at our tasks, as becomes serfs whose living is from the soil.

But tell me a thing that will likewise benefit you: with what
intent you have come this way. Is it Augeas you seek,   30
    or one of his servants, the men that he owns? If I knew this
        clearly,
I would direct you aright, for I vouch you are sprung of no
base stock; you have not grown like to one baseborn—
so great and noble your mien! Truly, I warrant, 'tis sons
of gods bear themselves so among mortal men!'
In answer to him then spake the stalwart son of Zeus:
'Yea, old man, I would see Augeas, the Epeans' chieftain;
    for that it is I have come; but if care for his people detains
        him
    in town with his burghers, hearing suits, do you name me
        an elder
among his house-slaves, the senior man in charge   40
    of these fields, and lead me to him, that of him I may
        inquire
and be answered: god makes man to stand in need of man!'
Him the ancient, the worthy ploughman answered again:
'Friend, by the counsel of some god hither have you come,
so all your will is set on shall straightway be fulfilled.
For here is Augeas, own son to Helios, arrived
but yesterday from town, with son of his, the illustrious
Prince Phyleus. He comes after many moons to view
the gains accruing countless in his fields. It seems
even the minds of kings perceive their households safer   50
for their own overseeing. But let us be going to him.
I will lead you to our stable, where you may find my lord.'
So saying he led the way, but laboured much in his mind,
seeing the lion's skin and the club that filled his grasp,
over the stranger's whence. Ever he thought to ask him,
but caught the speech back to his lips even as it left them,
in shame lest he utter some word untimely to one in haste,
for hard it is to know the mind of another man.
As they approached—they were still far off—immediately
    the dogs
    got wind of them, from their scent and the sound of their
        footfall, both,   60

and raising a rare howling, rushed this way and that,
upon Heracles, son of Amphitryon, and surrounded the
    old man
with idle yelps and fawnings. He sent them skulking back
by merely lifting stones from the ground, and with harsh
    voice
hurling threats at them all, he put a stop to their howling;
but in his thoughts he was glad, seeing they guarded the
    stalls
even when he was not by. This, though, was what he said:
'Too bad, that the lord gods made such a beast
as man's companion, acting before it thinks! Had it equal
70 wit to discern, it would know who to resent, who not;
nor would any of the beasts contend with it for worth.
But as things are it's too touchy and downright snarling a
    creature!'
So much—and with no more delay they went their way to
    the stable.

The Visit to the Stable

Then Helios turned his horses toward the dusk and led
the late day on, and the fat flocks returned
coming back from the pasture to the sheepfolds and the
    pens:
the many thousand cattle, drove on drove as they passed,
appeared like water-laden clouds that are seen in the sky,
driven before the might of Notus or Thracian Boreas—
80 clouds, of which, as they travel the air, is neither number
nor end, so many the force of the wind sends rolling after
the foremost, and others the while are rearing crest upon
    crest:
even so many the cattle followed, herd upon herd:
the whole plain and all the paths were filled with livestock
moving along; the fertile fields overflowed with lowing.
The pens rapidly filled with heavy-footed cattle;
the sheep were lodged in their folds. Then none stood idly
    beside

the kine; though the hands were countless, none lacked
   work.
but one tied hobbles around their feet with leather thongs
and came close to milk; another loosed the newborn calves,   90
who sped with one mind under their dams to drink
the mild milk. One held a pail, another set curds
for cheese, and another led in the bulls apart from the cows.
Augeas went through all, observing the stalls and the store
of goods his herdsmen had laid up for him, and with him his
   son
and mighty Heracles, deep in thought, following the king
as he viewed his great wealth. Amphitryon's son, though
   he kept
his thoughts checked in his breast, ever and constantly
   close,
yet wondered exceedingly seeing the myriad gift of the
   god.
None would have guessed or expected so great a prize
   would fall   100
to one man—not to ten beside, though wealthiest among kings.
Helios made this signal gift to his son, to be worth
more cattle than all other men, and to him he owed them
   entirely,
right to the last. Not only did no sickness stalk his flocks,
such as spoils the herdsman's labours; rather his horned
   oxen
increased, nay improved, year in, year out; truly the cows
all brought forth alive and in plenty and female withal.
Together with these were ranked three hundred bulls: black
with white shanks and another two hundred red, all studs
already. And beside these was another herd of twelve   110
sacred to Helios; their colour was like the silver white
of swans; they shone among all the cattle and spurred the
   herd
as they browsed the verdant pasture-grass, lording it over
   the rest
with threatening mien; and whenever out of the wild woods

swift beasts of prey appeared on the plain in search
of the beasts of the field, these would be the first to start
battleward along the track of their scent and bellow
fearfully, with murderous looks upon their brows. Of these
the great Phaethon was foremost in might and muscle and
    swagger,
120 whom all the herdsmen likened to a star, because as he went
among the other cattle, he gleamed in brilliant form.
He, on seeing the stiff hide of the staring lion,
straight rushed on the wary Heracles himself and brushed
his head and stubborn brow against his flanks. As he
    charged,
the hero took his left horn in the unrelenting grip
of his broad hand, and downward bore the neck to the
    ground,
massive though it was, and thrust him back behind him
with the force of his shoulder: around the sinew his
    straining muscles
stood out from the top of his arm. The king himself and his
    son,
the thoughtful Phyleus, and they who had charge of the
130   horned kine,
marvelled on seeing the monstrous strength of
    Amphitryon's son.

Heracles and the Lion

So on for the town, leaving the fertile fields, they fared,
Phyleus and mighty Heracles, in single file, and gained
the spot where first they set foot on the highway, after
    traversing
with rapid steps the narrow trail which stretched between
the vineyards and the steading, and was none too clear to
    see
for the green overhang. And there Augeas' son
addressed the offspring of high Zeus who followed behind,
turning his head a little over his right shoulder:

'Friend, my mind has been running just now on a tale that I
    heard   140
long since about you—if you it was. There came
travelling hither from Argos—I was quite a child—
a man of Achaea, from Helix beside the sea, who said—
and many Epeans heard him say as much—that an Argive
slew, as he was witness, a beast, a monstrous lion,
dread scourge of the countryside, which laired in a cave
by the grove of Nemean Zeus. "I know not for sure if he
    came
from holy Argos itself or dwelt in the city of Tiryns
or Mycene." These were his words, and he added the descent
(if rightly I recall) of the hero was from Perseus.   150
I've a suspicion no other of the Achaeans dared this thing
but you, and the lion's skin that drapes your sides proclaims,
with certainty, the mighty deed of your hands. Come, now,
    Sir,
say first that I may know in all conscience, whether or not
I truly divine that you are he of whom we heard
the Achaean from Helix tell, and whether I name you aright.
Then tell how this beast of bane you slew with your bare
    hands
and how it came to the well-watered country of Nemea.
So great a monster I warrant you would not find in all Apis,
even should you wish, for none it supports of such size,   160
but only bears and boars and the cursed breed of wolves.
They wondered who heard the story and some said it was
    but the lies
of a tramp with an idle tongue to tell tales to his boon-
    companions!'
As he spoke, Phyleus vacated the crown of the road, that
    they might
have space to walk side by side and he the more easily
hear what Heracles had to say, who answered him thus:
'O son of Augeas, that which you asked me first, yourself
full easily have surmised, going straight to the mark. I can
    tell you

each circumstance surrounding this monster as it befell—
since you have wished to hear—save where it came from; for that
170 could none of the Argives, though many, plainly declare.
    We only
guessed that one of the holy immortals, wroth with the sons
of Phoroneus, loosed this scourge; for like a river bursting
on all its valley-dwellers, the lion laid pitiless waste,
and most of all to the Bembinaeans who, neighbours to his
    range,
suffered beyond enduring. This was the first labour
Eurystheus laid upon me to fulfill. He bade me kill
the fearsome beast, and I set out taking my supple bow
and hollow quiver filled with arrows: in the other hand,
180 my stout staff, a thickset olive, its bark still on,
and the pith in its core, which finding under sacred Helicon,
myself had pulled up, thick roots and all. So when
I reached the lion's terrain, I took my bow and fitted
the string to its curved horns and straight set it about
the sorrow-dealing arrows. I was casting my eyes about,
spying out the baneful monster and hoping to get my sights
on him before he on me. It was midday and yet could I not
observe his tracks nor hear his roar; nor was any man
to be seen with his oxen or labouring, through all the sown
    ploughland,
190 of whom I might inquire. Pale fear held all
in their homesteads. In truth, I never checked my feet; I
    searched
the thick-leaved mountainside until I saw him, and straight
made trial of my strength. For late in the day he would go to
    his cave,
having gorged on meat and blood; around his squalid mane
and glaring face and breast was spattered the carnage; his
    tongue
licked his chops. I had hidden myself in the shade of some
    bushes

on a woodland path, waiting until he should come. As he
   passed,
swiftly I loosed an arrow at his left flank—in vain!
The weapon held not its course through the ridged flesh,
   but rebounded
and fell on the green sward. Though astonished, he quickly
   reared   200
his bloody head from the ground, spying all about
with searching eyes and snarling showed his wicked teeth.
Vexed that my first had idle scaped my hand, I sent
a second dart from the string; it struck him full in the chest,
the very seat of the lungs; even so the pain-dealing
arrow failed to pierce below the hide but fell
in front of his paws, equally useless. A dreadful loathing
seized me as the third time I prepared to draw
and the eyes of the monstrous beast, as they rolled round,
   sighted me.
He lashed his long tail about his loins and his mind   210
ran upon battle; his throat swelled all with spleen;
with ire bristled his tawny mane; his spine bent
like a bow as he gathered his length below his flanks and
   midriff.
As a chariot-maker, man of many skills, will bend
shoots of pliant figwood, warmed first in the fire,
as wheels for axled cars—but the long withy scapes
from under the hands that bend it and leaps away at a bound:
so the terrible lion arched himself and sprang
from far upon me, raging to taste my flesh. I held
in one hand my darts and the cloak from my shoulders,
   folded;   220
with the other I swung my seasoned club about my ears
and smashed it down on his head, but split the wild olive,
rugged as it was, asunder on the invincible brute's
maned skull. Before he could come at me, he fell,
dropping down on the ground and stood on trembling feet
swaying his head, for darkness swam about his eyes

swaying his head, for darkness swam about his eyes
at the stunning shock to the brain's core. Seeing him witless
with whelming pain, before he could turn and breathe again,
I was quick to advance and seize him by the scruff of his
    iron neck,
having thrown my bow to the ground with my broidered
230   quiver. Then
I throttled him mightily with my stout hands, reaching round
from behind lest he lacerate my flesh with his claws. I set
solidly my heels on his hind feet and pressed them down
to the ground—my knees took care of his sides—until I raised
his body up breathless in my arms and stretched it out.
Dire Hades received his life. My next perplexity
was to draw the shaggy hide from the dead beast's limbs:
a very taxing labour, for to attempt it I had
neither knife of iron nor stone nor other means.
240   Then a god put it into my head to slit the lion's skin
with the lion's own claws; with these I soon had it off
and wrapped it around my frame to serve as a shield against
the cut and thrust of the battle-rout. And there, my friend,
you have the tale of the fate that befell the lion of Nemea,
that was once the cause of many a sorrow to flocks and to
    men.'

✿ Bibliography

A complete bibliography of books and articles about Theocritus that were written up until 1952 appears in A. S. F. Gow, *Theocritus: Edited with a Translation and Commentary*, vol. 2, *Commentary, Appendix, Indexes, and Plates* (Cambridge: At the University Press, 1952), pp. 561–94. My select bibliography below is intended to provide further guidance to work on Theocritus completed after 1952. I have listed all the books and articles to which I have referred in my text, as well as a number of other studies of particular value to the reader of Theocritus as a poet. My selection is weighted in favour of the English-speaking reader, though a number of important works in other languages are also listed.

GENERAL STUDIES ON THEOCRITUS OR OF PARTICULAR INTEREST TO THE READERS OF THEOCRITUS

Books

Beck, W. A. 'Theocritus' Use of Literary Symbolism'. Ph.D. dissertation, Stanford University, 1973.

Boyle, A. J., ed. *Ramus* 4 (1975). A special issue 'devoted to the Ancient Pastoral', containing papers by Harriet Edquist, Gilbert W. Lawall, and Charles Segal.

Cairns, Francis. *Generic Composition in Greek and Roman Poetry*. Edinburgh: Edinburgh University Press, 1971.

Dover, K. J. *Theocritus: Select Poems Edited with an Introduction and Commentary*. London: Macmillan, 1971.

Köhnken, Adolf. *Apollonios Rhodios und Theokrit*. Hypomnemata: Untersuchungen zur Antike und zu ihren Nachlebens, vol. 12. Göttingen: Vandenhoeck and Ruprecht, 1965.

Lawall, Gilbert W. *Theocritus' Coan Pastorals: A Poetry Book*. Publications of the Center for Hellenic Studies, vol. 1. Washington, Center for Hellenic Studies, 1967.

Nicosia, Salvatore. *Teocrito e l'arte figurata*. Quaderni dell'Istituto di filologia greca dell'Università di Palermo, vol. 5. Palermo, 1968.

Ott, Ulrich. *Die Kunst des Gegensatzes in Theokrits Hirtengedichten*. Spudasmata: Studien zur Klassischen Philologie und ihren Grenzgebieten, vol. 22. Hildesheim: G. Olms, 1969.

Rosenmeyer, T. G. *The Green Cabinet: Theocritus and the European Pastoral Tradition*. Berkeley and Los Angeles: University of California Press, 1969.

Serrao, Gregorio. *Problemi di poesia alessandrina I: Studi su Teocrito*. Filologia e critica, vol. 8. Rome: Edizioni dell'Ateneo, 1971.

Webster, T. B. L. *Hellenistic Poetry and Art*. London: Methuen, 1964.

General Articles

Campbell, Malcolm. 'Three Notes on Alexandrian Poetry'. *Hermes* 102 (1974):38–46.

Dick, B. F. 'Ancient Pastoral and the Pathetic Fallacy'. *Comparative Literature* 20 (1968):27–44.

Garson, R. A. 'Formal Aspects of Theocritean Comparisons'. *Classical Quarterly* 68 (1972):103–6.

Irigoin, J. 'Les Bucoliques de Théocrite: La composition du recueil'. *Quaderni Urbinati di cultura classica* 19 (1975):27–44.

Segal, Charles. 'Death by Water: A Narrative Pattern in Theocritus (Idylls, 1, 13, 22, 23)'. *Hermes* 102 (1974):20–38.

Smutny, R. J. 'The Text History of the Epigrams of Theocritus'. *University of California Publications in Classical Philology* 15 (1955):29–34.

STUDIES OF INDIVIDUAL POEMS

I

Ogilvie, R. M. 'The Song of Thyrsis'. *Journal of Hellenic Studies* 82 (1962):106–10.

Segal, Charles. 'Since Daphnis Dies: The Meaning of Theocritus' First Idyll'. *Museum Helveticum* 3 (1974):1–22.

Schmidt, E. A. 'Die Leiden des verliebten Daphnis'. *Hermes* 96 (1968): 539–52.

Zuntz, Günther. 'Theocritus I. 95f.' In his *Opuscula Selecta*, pp. 83–87. Manchester: University of Manchester Press, 1972; also in *Classical Quarterly* 10 (1960):37–40.

II

Lawall, Gilbert W. 'Simaetha's Incantation: Structure and Imagery'. *Transactions of the American Philological Association* 92 (1961): 283–94.

Rist, Anna. 'The Incantatory Sequence in Theocritus' Pharmaceutria'. *Maia* 27 (1975):103–11.

Segal, Charles. 'Simaetha and the Iynx'. *Quaderni Urbinati di cultura classica* 15 (1973):32–43.

III

Segal, Charles. 'Adonis and Aphrodite: Theocritus, Idyll III 48'. *Acta Classica* 38 (1969):82–88.

IV

Barigazzi, Adelmo. 'Per l'interpretazione e la datazione del carme IV di Teocrito'. *Rivista di filologia e di istruzione classica* 102 (1974):301–11.

Giangrande, Giuseppe. 'Theocritus' Twelfth and Fourth Idylls: A Study in Hellenistic Irony'. *Quaderni Urbinati di cultura classica* 12 (1971):95–113.

Lattimore, S. 'Battus in Theocritus' Fourth Idyll'. *Greek, Roman and Byzantine Studies* 14 (1973):319–24.

Lawall, Gilbert W. 'Theocritus' Fourth Idyll: Animal Loves and Human Loves'. *Rivista di filologia e di istruzione classica* 94 (1966): 42–50.

Segal, Charles. 'Theocritean Criticism and the Interpretation of the Fourth Idyll'. *Ramus* 1 (1972):1–25.

Sickle, J. B. van. 'The Fourth Pastoral Poems of Virgil and Theocritus'. *Atti e memorie dell'Arcadia*, ser. 3, vol. 5 (1969):1–20.

V

Schmidt, E. A. 'Der gottliche Ziegenhirt: Analyse des fünften Idylls als Beitrag zu Theokrits bukolischer Technik'. *Hermes* 102 (1974): 207–43.

Serrao, Gregorio. 'L'idyllio V di Teocrito: Realtà campestre e stilizzazione letteraria'. *Quaderni Urbinati di cultura classica* 19 (1975):73–110.

VII

Cameron, Archibald. 'The form of the Thalysia'. In *Miscellanea di studi Alessandrini in memoria di Augusto Rostagni*, pp. 291–307. Turin: B. d'Erasmo, 1963.

Giangrande, Giuseppe. 'Théocrite, Simichidas et les "Thalysies"'. *Antiquité classique* 37 (1968):508–11.

Kühn, J. H. 'Die Thalysien Theokrits'. *Hermes* 86 (1958):40–79.

Luck, Georg. 'Zur Deutung von Theokrits Thalysien'. *Museum Helveticum* 23 (1966):186–89.

Ott, Ulrich. 'Theokrits Thalysien und Ihre literarischen Vorbilder'. *Rheinisches Museum* 115 (1972):134–49.

Puelma, M. 'Die Dichterbegegnung in Theokrits "Thalysien"'. *Museum Helveticum* 17 (1960):144–64.

Segal, Charles. 'Simichidas' Modesty: Theocritus, Idyll 7, 44'. *American Journal of Philology* 95 (1974):128–36.

————. 'Theocritus' Seventh Idyll and Lycidas'. *Wiener Studien* 8 (1974):20–76.

X

Cairns, Francis. 'Theocritus' Idyll x'. *Hermes* 98 (1970):38–44.

Whitehorne, J. B. G. 'The Reapers: Theocritus Idyll 10'. *A.U.M.L.A.: Journal of the Australasian Universities' Modern Language Association* 41 (1974): 30–49.

XI

Barigazzi, Adelmo. 'Una presunta aporia nel c. 11 di Teocrito'. *Hermes* 103 (1975):179–88.

Brooke, A. C. 'Theocritus' Idyll 11: A Study in Pastoral'. *Arethusa* 4 (1971): 73–81.

Holtsmark, E. B. 'Poetry as Self-enlightenment: Theocritus xi'. *Transactions of the American Philological Association* 97 (1966):253–59.

Spoffard, E. W. 'Theocritus and Polyphemus'. *American Journal of Philology* 90 (1969):22–35.

XIII

Latte, Kurt. 'Zu Theokrits Hylas'. In *Festschrift Bruno Snell zum 60 Geburtstag*, pp. 25–28. Munich: C. H. Beck'sche, 1956.

Mastronarde, D. J. 'Theocritus' Idyll 13: Love and Hero'. *Parola del passato* 23 (1968):5–18 and *Transactions of the American Philological Association* 99 (1968):273–90.

XIV

Stern, J. 'Theocritus' Idyll 14'. *Greek, Roman and Byzantine Studies* 16 (1975):51–58.

XV

Swigart, R. 'Theocritus' Pastoral Response to City Women'. *Bucknell Review* 21 (1973):145–74.

XVI

Austin, J. N. H. 'Theocritus and Simonides'. *Transactions of the American Philological Association* 98 (1967):1–21.

XXII

Hagopian, D. *Pollux' Faustkampf mit Amykos*. Stuttgart: Braumüller, 1955.

Moulton, Carroll. 'Theocritus and the Dioscuri'. *Greek, Roman and Byzantine Studies* 14 (1973): 41–47.

XXVI

Carrière, J. 'Théocrite et les Bacchantes'. *Pallas* 6 (1958): 7–19.

————. 'Sur le message des Bacchantes'. *Acta Classica* 35 (1966):118–39.

McKay, K. J. 'Theokritos' Bacchantes Re-examined'. *Antichthon* 1 (1967):16–28.

Valk, M. H. van der. 'Theocritus 26'. *Acta Classica* 34 (1965):84–96.

Van Groningen, B. A. 'Les Bacchantes de Théocrite'. In *Miscellanea di studi Alessandrini in memoria di Augusto Rostagni*, pp. 338–49. Turin: B. d'Erasmo, 1963.

✤ Index

A NOTE ON THE AUTHOR

Anna Rist, educated at Newnham College, Cambridge, has taught English and classics at North London Collegiate School and has been lecturer in the classics department of St. Michael's College, University of Toronto.

A NOTE ON THE BOOK

Composed by The University of North Carolina Press in Mergenthaler VIP Bembo

Printed on sixty-pound Warren's Olde Style

Cover stock, Roxite Linen B 53561, by The Holliston Mills, Incorporated

Printing and binding by Edwards Brothers, Ann Arbor, Michigan

Designed by Martha Farlow

Published by The University of North Carolina Press